Violent Disorder

**A novel
by
Mark Barry**

Violent Disorder
Published by Green Wizard 2013
© Green Wizard 2013

This book is sold subject to the condition that it shall not by way of trade or otherwise, be lent, resold, hired out, or otherwise circulated without Green Wizard's prior permission and consent in any form of e-transaction, format, binding or cover other than that in which it is published and without a similar condition, including this condition, being imposed on the subsequent purchaser.

First published in 2013 by Green Wizard
Green Wizard, Southwell, Nottinghamshire
Greenwizard62@blogspot.com

Cover design by Dark Dawn Creations

This is a work of fiction. Any resemblance of characters to actual persons, living or dead, is purely coincidental.

ISBN-13: 978-1491239452
ISBN-10: 149123945X

Acknowledgements

Major thanks are due to Mary Ann Bernal, my editor and friend, who pointed out the things that needed pointing out about my writing, and who worked tirelessly to make sure this was the kind of work it was meant to be. She polished it up a treat and deserves major credit for the tireless work she does. We don't always agree, and we can sometimes have, what the characters in this book might call a *major off,* but she does it for the best and without her, the reading experience you are about to have wouldn't be as tight, as sharp and as polished as I hope it is going to be.

Thanks, Mary Ann.

Andrew, Tony, Mary and Patricia Barry continue to support the enterprise as well as my other stuff.

And from the early days, I still have friends rooting for me in the background, chief among them being Kelly Sherwood.

I'd also like to thank brilliant children's author, Ngaire Victoria Elder, and St Louis reader, Mary Quallo, who buy everything I write, offering their support and constructive criticism. I am sure they will do the same here.

Finally, I'd also like to thank the large numbers of people who bought, borrowed or downloaded *Ultra Violence.*

You are the reason the gang are back.

Novels by Mark Barry

Carla
Hollywood Shakedown
Kid Atomic
The Illustrated Woman
The Ritual
Ultra Violence
Violent Disorder

Green Wizard Anthology

Reality Bites

Introduction

For those of you who ignore introductions and get straight into the *meat,* please don't ignore this one – it has a football violence themed nugget of history embedded within.

You don't want to miss that, do you?

My name is Mark Barry, and I am a writer.

I write fiction (and other things).

I have written six novels, including horror *(The Ritual),* a quest novel *(Hollywood Shakedown),* a dark romance *(Carla),* and a work in a genre of my own invention, social commentary and erotica *(The Illustrated Woman).* None of which have sold anywhere near as many as my tale of football hooliganism at a small but prestigious, Midlands football club.

That book is called *Ultra Violence* and you can find it on Amazon. I'd buy it if I were you before you read this – it's cheap and introduces all the characters you'll find in here.

For those of you who are picking up *Violent Disorder* without reading *Ultra Violence,* the club in question is Notts County. I also support the club. Ninety percent of the time, I wish I didn't. Can there be another pastime where most of the spectators wish they were somewhere else? I am a passionate horseracing enthusiast and can be found every meeting at Southwell Races, and even on those days where I end up that broke that it's necessary to walk home, I always enjoy the experience of racing. I go to the flicks – I write this the day after seeing *Man of Steel* on IMAX, and it was worth every penny. Music, comics, books (obviously), the environment, and beekeeping are some of my other passions, and I love all of them – but Notts? *Notts?* Following Notts County tests your loyalty to the brink. Witnessing these fellows in action, I partly understood why they sought to make their Saturday afternoon a bit more entertaining because generally, the football they were asked to pay large amounts of money to see just wasn't worth it. It still isn't. Putting the little blue envelope into the collection plate seems a fair analogy of being a Notts fan – a duty, a sense of being part of something – and these fellows were not the type to sit and listen to a tedious sermon delivered by a near-dead white male in a black dress.

The book you are about to read is a loose sequel to *Ultra Violence.* It contains all new stories. In the first book, I recount the incident at home to Luton, described in *Ultra Violence* (the *Last Match of the Season*), but I was being led away by my father as fans of the two clubs attacked each other with relish. Dad offered a serious, and unprintable, moral commentary on the hooligans scooting past us on London Road, intent on battering the other side's supporters to a pulp. He didn't take me to Chelsea away or to Hartlepool in the FA Cup; matches considered by just about all the people I spoke to as the scariest matches any Notts fan could have attended in the eighties.

My research into the genre revealed more moral positions than a garden party at a Tory MP's moated castle. *Steaming In*, Colin Ward's groundbreaking hooligan novel is spoiled by the apologia running through the latter chapters like a seam of coal through an Appalachian mountainside. Jay Allan's earthy and atavistic *Diary of a Football Hooligan* is a tale of Scottish Presbyterianism concealed by a Tacchini tracksuit. The Brimson Brothers, old school opportunists, hagiographers and exploiters of the hooligan genre, seem to have negotiated publishing deals where it is incumbent upon them to write "we do not condone the activities in this book" at least fifteen times. Mercifully, the Cass Pennant/Martin King tomes don't appear to be subject to the same moral code. Nor on another literary level entirely, was John King and his brilliant *Kings Road* trilogy, which starts with the most famous hooligan book of all, *The Football Factory,* the benchmark for any writer of football hooligan tales.

I don't offer any apologies. I wasn't there, am merely the biographer, and it is up to the readers to impose a moral framework. Or not, as the case may be.

My first up close encounter with Notts County's hooligans came by sheer coincidence at the last game of the season in 2004. I watched some of them in action on London Road, outside the Norfolk Pub (now, like all the pubs along the old industrial district, sadly defunct, leaving the brash and tacky Hooters joint underneath the Hickings and Pentecost building, which seems to cater exclusively to away supporters).

Due to attendance at a christening, I was late for the match versus Oldham Athletic. I was on my way to see the second half, and arrived on the road at the same time as ten men who had seemingly left the old Hooters, the one opposite the Holmes Place gym.

I remember it being a stifling day. The long tributary bridge over the river Trent was relatively empty of cars and the sun beat relentlessly with no comforting breeze. The canal reflected the sun's rays like a mirror; only the lures and flies of the many anglers peacefully lining the canal disturbed the reflective patina.

The ten men's ages ranged from sixteen to forty, at a glance, and they walked faster than I, offering no threat to me as they passed. Subconsciously or not, I speeded up slightly and kept up with them.

As I walked, I was thinking about my sister, Wendy, and whether or not her marriage to Gerry would survive, when on the other side of the road, I noticed a large number of men emerging from the old Norfolk pub. Instinctively, I knew they were football lads – not a stag party or a union meeting on a fag break.

They were a firm, and I suspected they were a rival firm.

Tracksuit tops, trainers, jeans, caps. When I spoke to some of the participants seven years later, I discovered that they were Oldham's top boys – including an organiser for the England firm who was allegedly prominent in the inglorious riot at Lansdowne Road against the Republic of Ireland. A "name".

I tensed. We were on the canal side of the road, twenty five yards away, but I was close enough to the ten men to be considered the eleventh member of the gathering. A mob, who I realised simultaneously, must have been a small firm of Notts avoiding the nothing-to-play-for encounter two hundred yards away, the giant Kop stand visible over the hill.

As a result, I slowed down. It occurred to me that with no policemen about, there was going to be a fight.

Notts were outnumbered about two to one.

Oldham stayed as if anchored by a tractor beam in a semi-circular shape around the front door of the Norfolk. The locals on the canal side of the road started to bait the Northwesterners, seemingly oblivious to the fact they weren't favoured by the odds. In Burberry, Hackett caps and Adidas trainers, the two gangs began to go at it. The locals didn't seem to notice me, and I kept my head down, staring at the pavement for dear life. Like cave dwellers, I felt the two gangs were symbolically displaying their five hundred quid chemise jackets like plumage. Beating their chests; in other words, symptomatic of a territorial dispute.

I noticed two older men, one of who resembled Tony Iommi out of Black Sabbath, an incongruous figure in context, with no sportswear brands to display; a jeans combo, hair reaching his shoulders, a goatee beard, and big black biker boots.

The more I look back at that, the more he looked like Dimebag out of Pantera – shorter than Tony, more squat, the same build as Maradona. Next to him, hanging back from the herd slightly was a taller man, built in the parlance, like a barn door. He was better dressed than the rocker standing next to him, who it seemed to me, had seemingly spent the night in the industrial skips outside Eastcroft Incinerator, an allegorical hotel popular with Nottingham's homeless; when they can get in.

The two men stood there like hawks in the background, leaning on London Road's railings. Assessing the situation while the two younger mobs ruminated, pointed, grunted and gestured – the universal gesture for *come on then* – arms extended forward, palms reversed, fingers close together, bending quickly and repeatedly backwards – then, explosively, unexpectedly, I heard the words "Fuck this".

Fuck this.

I remember hearing it distinctively, even if it wasn't intended to be heard, not quite a whisper, definitely not a shout, the words hanging in the tranquil air above the canal like the retort from a shotgun.

It was Dimebag.

The two men, tired of the phony war and all the coquettish display (and quite out of the blue), started to run at the platoon of Oldham over the road.

Confident I wasn't considered part of all this, and in order to observe, I stood and leaned on the barrier between the road and the canal ten feet below. My heart raced. I was thrilled by what I saw. Dimebag and his taller heavier friend running across the road. On cue, the rest of the Notts followed shouting, and I expected, like at Hastings, or Poitiers, the men-at-arms to clash in the middle of the battlefield, but they didn't.

The Oldham phalanx, twice the number and noticeably shocked at the presence of the dynamic duo racing towards them, began to retreat.

I think I would have done as well. I'm not being critical of them.

Dimebag's bizarre sprinting ability would have been something else to confront head-on – a Viking disembarking his longship on Scarborough beach, racing up the rocks toward the monastery, a double-headed bloodaxe swinging above his head – and it visibly had an unsettling effect on Oldham, who clearly didn't expect this to happen.

And they ran. All of them.

Broke ranks and ran.

The leader of the platoon, blonde, lean and wiry, in a white tracksuit top – evidently the top man, the England bloke – implored his mob to stand, but Dimebag was heading straight for him like a hairy Exocet, and he wasn't going to stop. He would have run *straight through* the Oldham top man had he stood there.

Heavily outnumbered by the onrushing Notts mob, the Oldham top man started to run with his friends, but even I could see it was with some reluctance. He was the type of warrior who would rather die with his sword in his hand than with an arrow in his back as he retreated into the dark woods.

Unlike his friends.

The local ten chased the retreating Oldham all the way back to the ground and then, in the blink of an eye as the sound of sirens filled the air, they were gone, like mist, through the trees lining the far side of London Road, into the alleys, ginnels and side streets of the Meadows.

Later – seven years later – I was told the name of those two friends.

Actually brothers.
The Bully brothers[1].

I got to know four or five of the others in that victorious mob. Some of them appear in the book you are about to read.

---

[1] For the purpose of the book – and I'm not giving anything away in the plot by telling you that the remainder of the book is mostly about these two brothers, now well into their forties – I have changed their names. In *Ultra Violence*, they were known as Older Bully and Younger Bully. Over a sixty thousand word novel that might amount to a thousand extra words, so the defenestration of their names is entirely wise and practical. For a leaner reading experience, the older one is called HobNob and the younger one is called Bull. There are other reasons for the name change, but the brevity angle is the best one.

It is, like *Ultra Violence*, in the end, a work of fiction, loosely based on ancient tales and campfire stories. It should be treated as such.

I hope you enjoy it.

Mark Barry
Southwell

"The sombre fact is that we are the cruellest and most ruthless species that has ever walked the earth; and that, although we may recoil in horror when we read of the atrocities committed by man on man, we know in our hearts, that each one of us harbours within ourselves those same savage impulses, which lead to murder, to torture and to war." (Anthony Storr)

The most dangerous creation of any society
is the man with nothing to lose.
(James Baldwin)

Little County.
County's got no lads.
Little County.
Wankers, County.
Old men.
Got no lads.
Who the fuck are Notts County.
Little County.
County's got no lads...

(Trad: *Pub Gossip*: Circa late twentieth,
early twenty first century.)

1. Cedar Forest

The car pulled up in front of me and by extension, the pub wall, and I stood, zipped up my coat and ambled over. A six year old Citroen saloon, silver.

Alright, I said, in greeting, as he rolled down the window.

He nodded in return and gestured me in. The car was neat and smelt of Car Duck air freshener, and I noticed the duck symbol, pink, corpulent, hanging off the mirror, the place where the furry dice should be.

You could eat scrambled eggs off the upholstery: Jet-black, profusely fibred and dust free. Music played, and I recognised it straight away.

Jake Bugg. *Lightning Bolt.*

Without further comment, he looked over his shoulder and pulled away from the kerb. I glanced over. I hardly knew him and his e-mail to me came as something of a surprise. I'd not seen him at the Lane recently, though that is not to say he hadn't been there: A cavernous place like Meadow Lane is easy to hide in if you want to – or need to – and the people you usually want to avoid are creatures of habit, clinging to the same ranks of seats like sticklebricks.

However, I had been told he'd attended – old habits, like creatures with shells, die hard. Following Notts, ailing Notts County, forever wounded, forever bleeding, yet proudly the oldest football league club in the world was the hardest habit of all to leave aside for many of us.

Where are we headed? I asked, more to break the ice than anything.

Top end of Newark. Collingham. Do you know it?

No.

It's not far. About forty minutes.

I'm in no hurry, I replied, and that was true.

It was Sunday, a Sunday in March. Winter had shown no sign of passing through. There was a touch of frost outside, and the skies were metallic grey, pregnant with snow. Much of the country had fallen victim to the snow, but the East Midlands missed it sometimes, like now. It had been a dreadful winter and like a dull guest at a birthday party, it showed no sign of taking its leave.

Inside the car was all heat, and I loosened my quilted jacket. We drove up past Nottingham Racecourse, past the sprawling Colwick Industrial Estate – the herald of destruction for ten thousand acres of virgin Nottinghamshire countryside – and past the beleaguered, Morrisons supermarket.

Traffic was light and we soon reached Burton Joyce. The two of us had hardly communicated since the pick-up and the atmosphere in the car was awkward and uneasy. He didn't take his eyes off the road. I wondered whether he was one of those drivers who had to concentrate, but I suspected that it wasn't like that at all: He was one of those men who didn't make small talk. Then, unexpectedly, as we passed the Magna Carta in Lowdham on one of the busiest rural crossroads in Notts, he asked me a question.

What do you think of the Forest revival, he asked.

I didn't need to think about it and responded immediately. It's going to be a nightmare if they are promoted, I replied.

Forest had recently recruited their old supremo Billy Davies and they were back on a run, winning game after game. The sight of the Reds winning turns Notts blood cold. If both teams struggled in the lower leagues, it wouldn't have mattered a jot, but with the whole country obsessed with the Premier League (all the blank faced plastics, all the pundits, all the media, all the TV, all the money, all the psychology), Forest in the EPL would be more than many Notts could take. Stan Collymore, Forest's ex-striker-turned-media-mouthpiece, said that he would love the existence of a smaller Premier League where every week Man Utd played Arsenal and Chelsea played Tottenham. Etcetera, etcetera.

Mouthwatering, he described it.

He wasn't alone in his opinion. Forest stood more of a chance than Notts did of ever being in that mythical supergroup. The prospect of their promotion this season was one that inspired genuine fear.

I'll have to go back out to Qatar or something, the driver said. No way would I stay in this country. It would be a bastard to live local. Imagine the Post. Imagine Radio Red....

There would be a mass exodus of Notts fans, definitely, I concurred.

Outside, it had begun to rain, but it was cold for just rain, for simple rain; it wouldn't just stay like that and I hoped this was just a squall. The driver smiled thinly as he continued.

Everyone is saying they want the cunts beat in the last minute of extra time of the playoff final, but nah, I can't risk them winning it. I want them to miss out on the playoffs altogether.

I think you're probably right.

Reedy, almost imperceptible lips, like bamboo, but the rest of him – his greying blonde hair and meaty cheeks, his tank-grey eyes flecked by a scar as insubstantial as his mouth; his blue fleece, his bulky frame – betrayed the fact that he was alarmed like the rest of us.

Our lives would not be worth living if Forest was promoted to the EPL. While they existed in the Sisyphean purgatory of Championship failure (boardroom incompetence, dismal management, mid-table, playoff defeat, repeat, repeat), life was bearable for a Notts County fan, but if they finally ascended...

I heard a funny story the other day, he said, interrupting my train of thought.

Did you?

I did. Do you want to hear it? It's about them cunts.

Okay.

This chap I know. Danny. That's his name. He was living in Sherwood. Do you know Haydn Road?

I do, I said.

Danny and his missus lived in a nice house behind the Quorn pub and the two of them lived there quite happily for years. Notts fan, big Notts fan. Home and away. Hated Forest with a passion you can't describe in words. Back in the nineties, he was pathological. In need of the intervention of a good psychiatrist. Hates them even now. Won't have Forest mates. Has no red items in his wardrobe. No red decoration in his house. Wouldn't let his missus wear red lipstick. Wouldn't even watch *films* with the title Red in it. *The Red Shoes. The Bride Wore Red. Code Red. Red Dawn. Red. Red Sonja*...no chance. Chromatically related films like *Crimson Tide*. Not a chance. This fella fucking hates Nottingham Forest Football Club. Couldn't give a monkey's whether Notts win or not, just as long as the Reds lose. Anyway, Dan and his missus went through some hard times, and they eventually decided to split up. He moved into lodgings as a trial separation and his missus kept the house. All amicable and they stayed friends. No one to blame, just one of those things. She soon realised that she can't afford the bills for the house, so she informs her ex that she is going to take in a lodger...

A lodger? Tricky...

I know, but it's that, or he would have to pay half the bills, so he gave her his blessing and before long, she had a lodger. Furthermore, as she's a tasty-looking woman, she found herself a fella. And because it's a nice house and her new fella lives in her old home town, she fell into the habit of asking Danny to housesit on a Saturday night.

What for?

As I said, it was a nice house in a dicey area – as you know, Sherwood started to decline badly in the midnineties, like everywhere else – and at that point, she didn't trust the lodger.

Okay, I see that.

Every second weekend or so, he went over to housesit, and on the second trip, he met the interloper. He was a fat fucker from Hull, no stranger to a fish supper or six. Big belly on him and jowls like a walrus. They got talking. The lodger told Danny that while he was into Rugby League, and since he was working in Nottingham, he might as well follow a football team as Nottingham is a rugby desert.

Danny asked politely who he planned to follow.

Mr Jowls said, with a big grin on his mush, who else! **Forest**! No *way* would I follow County, he said. Crap. Total bollocks. Where are they in the league? Muppets! They always lose. Who the fuck are County! How could I follow them? Got no fans and they're complete shit. How Danny didn't hit him, I don't know. In the end, it was fuck all to do with him, and he let it pass. He didn't want to plant his ex's new lodger because it would cost him eventually. The lodger was so self-absorbed that he didn't ask who Danny supports (or indeed, anything at all), and he moved on to talking about his shit taste in music, but Danny was seething inside.

I'll bet, I replied, absorbed.

Danny's ex went out one night up to Sheffield to see her new boyfriend, and he came over to housesit. Mr Jowls went out for the evening to watch the Panthers – Nottingham's ice hockey team as you know, a sport for cunts and wankers if ever there was one – and left Danny alone in his old gaff to go wandering, to see how the house has changed. He walked into the kitchen, and he saw it. The horror...

What?

There, next to the cooker – in *his* old house, the house *he* decorated, the house *he* furnished, the kitchen *he* painted meticulously, lovingly cared for – was a cheap Pound Goblin mug tree.

*And hanging from one of the branches was a **Tricky Trees mug.***

That's bad, I replied.

The Symbol of Satan. The Crimson Pentagram. The Red Tree of Mephistopheles.

That's bad. It hurts to listen to this story. Please stop.

Rather than smashing it, which would have been my choice, he removed it from the tree and sat staring at it. He stared at the mug for the longest time. Then, Eureka: He had an idea. He put the offending item back where it came from, picked up the phone, and called the local Indian. Ordered a Lamb Bhuna with all the trimmings. Plenty of keema and aloo, and Balti accompaniments. The meal soon arrived, and Danny snaffled the lot. I mean, the whole lot. Massive takeaway. Washed it down with four freezing-cold Stellas. Picked up the mug and took it with him into the front room and watched some shit Friday night TV. Before long, he was fast asleep on the sofa. When he woke up, he was ready. Felt his stomach. Heard it rumble. Saw the mug, picked it up and took it to the toilet. Took down his trousers and without further ado, bent over and evacuated most of his rancid, turmeric and lamb-tinged bowels into the mug. Filled it to the brim – indeed, the bhuna was so powerful an emetic, his diarrohetic effluvium spilled down the side – and left the mug in the bath. Went back downstairs to see the late night poker, or something, and waited. An hour later, he returned to the bathroom, picked up the mug, spooned the bubbling mass of his bowelly residue into the toilet where it belonged, ensuring a decent tobacco-brown glaze remained on the inside surface, went into his ex's bedroom and located her hairdryer. Turned the hairdryer on to max and dried the bhuna varnish, and just to make sure afterwards, he went downstairs and *microwaved* the mug. Inside the mug resembled a tea stain. Like a well sipped builder's mug. Carefully, he hung the mug on the tree, admired his handiwork one last time, and went to sleep on his old bed.

The next morning, Danny was woken by the smell of frying bacon. He knew it would be the lodger. He raced downstairs in his shorts and there he was, Mr Jowls, in his pinny.

I thought I'd make you some breakfast, he said jollily.

Great, Danny replied. Could murder a cuppa.

Oh, yes, the lodger said as he reached for the Tricky Trees mug on the kitchen table filled with Tetley tea, a legacy of his Yorkshire roots.

He leaned back on the sideboard and winked at Danny. Nothing like a fresh brewed cuppa first thing in t'morning, he said, winking, taking a big sip of morning refreshment, lovingly tinctured with Notts County blended bhuna shit.

I rolled with laughter.

The driver laughed, but not as hard. After all, he had heard it before.

Pulling over on a B road just north of Newark, a road I had never travelled, he wiped his nose on a serviette and gestured to a set of gates.

This is where we're going.

He pulled up in front of the gates. Giant gates with spear point tips ten feet across separating two pillars topped with alabaster leopards. I could see a brass plaque and I peered over to look. It said two words.

Cedar Forest.

Ironic, huh, the driver said.

In what sense?

In the sense of the story that I've just told you. I need to tell you another one, he said. He turned off the ignition and rested against the window.

I haven't spoken to him in ages. I'm not good with this kind of reunion stuff, and there's a possibility we could argue. You know how volatile he is. They say he's ready to come out, but you can never be sure. We're a bad influence on each other. We egg each other on.

Why me?

You wrote the book. You spoke to us. He likes you. He respects you. I'm not sure who else he respects. He's not going to kick off if you're about.

Why won't you tell me why he's here?

The driver shook his head. Because it is none of your business. Family stuff. It's enough that he's getting out. Anyways – thanks for coming.

You're welcome.

Keep an eye on him, the driver said to me, leaning over. I'm not sure how he's going to behave. He could be sound. He could be anything *but* sound.

He turned on the ignition key. The doors opened automatically, and the car drove up the pathway. Gravel crunched pleasingly underneath the car tyres. Acres of trees watched over us, forming a natural canopy, the shadows faint, the green lacklustre and specked with frost. Up ahead, I saw a building. Nineteenth Century, an old mansion, converted.

We pulled up into a car park, and the driver gestured to me. He took out an oversized organiser from the glove compartment stuffed with brown envelopes and turned to me.

Wait here. I won't be long, he said, and I wasn't going to argue. It was freezing outside, and it was warm in here, a no brainer.

I watched him walk up to the main doorway. Tall, thickset, powerful, a brutal presence that radiated, walking with a slight limp, an old wound, jeans, fleece, trainers – blue and white suede Forest Hills, or maybe Gazelles. He rang a bell and the mahogany coloured door (twice his height), opened automatically.

In he went.

I thought of the first time I met them in the Bentinck, the pub nearest the train station as I researched the book I was writing on Notts County football hooligans, the book that became *Ultra Violence*. I liked him. I liked both of them. They're easy to like. Intelligent. Cheerful. Knowledgeable. Supportive of the book. They helped me because they thought it was about time Notts had their own hooligan book. They answered their phones whenever I rang with a query or a quibble, and they were open and discursive. I went to the match with them a few times and I recorded their chatter, and they introduced me to their friends and acquaintances. Without them, I couldn't have done it. And when they read *Ultra Violence*, they couldn't have been kinder about the outcome.

The afternoon I first met them I was mindful of what people had said about *him*.

How he was volatile.

Likely to hit you for no reason.

Out of the blue.

How everyone was wary of him.

The eyes.

Black eyes.

Gelignite. An unstable material, which given the wrong set of circumstances could vibrate and go off with spectacular results.

The younger one was more predictable, a slow burner. Nice as pie unless you were an away fan. If you were a

Bradford fan, a Brighton fan, an Argyle fan, a Peterborough fan, or a Bristol Rovers fan, you wouldn't want to talk to him. You ought to stay away. The older one, he'd hit anyone. Anytime. For no apparent reason. Particularly plastic fans. While the younger one tended to hate anyone who came to Notts, the older one went for plastics – the people who watch Chelsea versus Tottenham in Sport Billy on a Sunday afternoon. Sky Sports junkies. Nottingham people who only consume football on TV. Fans of Man Utd who have never been to Manchester. Townies.

They said he was like an unexploded bomb.

That's what they said. Yet during our meetings, he was calm and peaceful. Never saw him give any trouble.

As I sat in the car, I wondered how he would be. In what mood. I wondered why he was in a place like this and what the purpose of the place was. I had my strong suspicions, but I didn't know for sure. I had seen enough horror films.

His brother wasn't saying, and I knew I would have to research Cedar Forest when I returned to Nottingham. I also couldn't work out why he had asked me to come along.

None of the reasons rang true with me, but I came anyway.

See the two of them together and you couldn't mistake the fact that they were brothers. The same walk, the same swagger. I watched them walk toward the car, the older one smaller, chunkier, in a tracksuit top, jeans and a pair of unbranded white tennis shoes, carrying a mountaineer's rucsac in which I assumed, were his clothes.

Evidently, the greeting between them had gone well. I could hear the crunch of the gravel, and I took that as my cue to get out of the car. I stood there, and the older one came up to me, an unreadable expression. He nodded at me without shaking my hand. I wondered whether the driver had told him why I was here and indeed, what he had told him. The reason given seemed an anaemic justification for me being there. I was not their friend; their biographer maybe, in the loosest sense – but not their friend.

We returned as a trio to the inside of the car, and the new arrival sat in the back next to his rucsac.

The crows don't roost at Auschwitz, he said.

Really? The driver replied, blank faced, focusing on the tree lined pathway down to the gates.

Yes, really. There's something about the place. The sheer horror. The sadness. Birds don't like it. The vibes. The aura. Not just crows: Other birds don't sing. You do see birdlife in the camp trees, but they do not call. And because the birds don't sing, there is a quietness reigning, a silence that remains un-replicated anywhere in the world. It seems, I have read, as if Auschwitz has been shunned by God Himself.

The driver looked at me askance. I returned the quizzical look.

And you're telling us this, why, he said.

His brother leaned forward, in-between the gap behind the front seats. I saw him, his angular protruding jaw, his barrel neck, his perfectly shaved chin, his spiky Stranglers style haircut, and his smirk, which could be interpreted a thousand ways. His eyes were as black as night (as usual), and for the first time, I noticed a gold sleeper in his left ear. He smelled of aftershave, but I couldn't place the brand.

This place, he replied. Cedar Forest. This hotel, which has been my home sweet home for eight months. Auschwitz reminds me of here. There is no difference. Cedar Forest. Auschwitz. Cedar Forest. Auschwitz. It's the same concept.

There's a world of difference, the driver replied, gesturing to the forest of oaks, and beeches, and the eponymous cedars on both sides. I definitely heard birds chirping earlier.

You never came to visit me; his brother interjected immediately, no gap, the subject change instant, appearing from nowhere.

I looked out of the window as we pulled up to the giant gates, more out of embarrassment than curiosity. The mood changed.

I've been in Tashkent. I couldn't visit, the driver said.

Good excuse.

The driver was having none of it. I could see him, demanding and flinty, the faint traces of a faded scar traversing his left eye socket.

You know the rules: It is every man for himself when it comes to football. Haxford's Law. Swindon. Remember Swindon?

Swindon. I remember...

Cost me seven hundred quid that weekend, including three hundred in a taxi.

In advance. Haxford doesn't take any prisoners on his coach. You're not there at the pick-up, you're history.

Breaker and The Printer nearly filled you in on the coach back for mithering the fuck out of everyone.

I was upset. You would have been upset. Watching your brother get nicked like that, two hundred miles away from home.

It was my fault. However, that's ancient history...

...ninety one?

Maybe the year after. The year the coppers started following us.

His brother leaned back in his seat and averred with an edge in his voice. Those Arnold copper cunts.

Those Arnold copper cunts, the driver repeated, parrot like. One of them cunts nicked us after Luton.

I know. I won't forget him. We'll meet up another time.

The younger brother did not attempt to drive through the gates. Keeping focused on some point in the distance, watching the cars pass on the main road perpendicular to the driveway. Transitory blurs, passing ephemera. He stared out of the windscreen keeping his hands firmly on the wheel. The atmosphere in the car ensured I found myself unconsciously pushing into the passenger door with my hips and side.

Families.

Brothers.

Conflict followed them round like camp servants.

The idea of divergence. The philosophy of violence.

I didn't expect this but then, coming along here, I didn't know what to expect.

The boiling atmosphere between the two of them pinged at my neck like a bully's finger flicking me on a coach trip from the seat directly behind.

I could feel the pressure rise; see the temperature gauge move to the red zone.

It was going to go off...

Anyway, do you want to make something of it? The driver said.

What do I want to make something of, brother?

My not visiting you because I was abroad for six months? You're not happy about it.

Do you want to make something of it?

Might do. I might do.

And all at once, the pressure released...

Let's do it, the driver said.

Before I could say anything, the two were out of the car. They started shouting, bawling, and the next thing I knew, they were wrestling on the road. Momentarily, I didn't know what to do, how to respond. This was family, but I made the decision anyway. Out of the passenger seat, I raced round to try and break up the fight.

When I did so, they stopped what they were doing. Stood up and laughed.

Relieved, I laughed, too.

Older Bully walked over to me and shook my hand.

Nice to see you. Glad you could come.

My pleasure.

We had you there, mate, Younger Bully said.

You pair used to scrap a lot.

We were kids. Come on, we have things to do.

The car absorbed us, and this time, the driver flicked the indicator and merged his car in with the speeding images.

2. Aunty Britney

On the journey back to Nottingham from Cedar Forest, we began to talk about Notts County – the third Bully brother if you like, the hidden member of their family, the ghost in the attic, the guilty secret that inspired their behaviour.

For a man recently released from an eight-month stretch in the country, Older Bully, whose nickname was HobNob, pattered away cheerfully as if his stay hadn't been much of a hardship. I sat there still wondering why he had been incarcerated in such a place. The fact I didn't know inspired in me the wildest speculations. He sat directly behind. Tracksuit top, jeans and trainers. He looked like a bloke just finished a shift in a sports warehouse.

Have I missed out this past year? He asked; his voice, heavily affected by a lifetime of smoking high-strength cigarettes (Bensons, Embassy, Marlboro). Like most people in UK, he had given up – something he was proud of.

Nothing. It's been the shittest season ever, Younger Bully, known as Bull, replied, turning onto the A1. You've not missed anything.

No action?

None. None at all.

Not even Rotherham?

Only amongst ourselves. Old uns and young uns in that nightclub next to the ground. Bitchslaps and diamante kisses.

Millers turn out?

We went looking beforehand, but it was quiet as a mouse.

I thought it would go off.

Coppers had it tucked up tight as a drum.

They always do.

Sea Monster found himself slapped afterwards by Henry M.

What for?

No idea. I was outside with Basford Paul having a wander about.

I saw that on the boards.

What, that I was having a wander about?

No, that Sea Monster got a slap.

Henry M hasn't been seen since. Imagine the Goggle Eyes in the morning.

Oh, my fucking god, HobNob says, snickering. I've been down that road many times. Jesus, *what have I DONE? What have I DONE!!*

Remember when you tried to snog your Chief Executive at that Board piss up.

HobNob laughed; put his head in his hands. Oh, my god. The morning after ... bloody hell ... never had wine since ... mind you, I quite fancied her. Is that it for the season then? Rotherham? Why turn on each other?

Happening all over the country. Used to be a taboo to fight with a member of your own team. Today? Common as muck.

Coppers?

Breakdown of modern society. No values whatsoever. Ever slapped a Notts fan?

Never. Unheard of in our day. Mind you...

What?

There was that time at Carlisle.

Oh, yes, Carlisle. Remember Sparks and the gang up at Rotherham...

...1988, four years after the Miners' Strike left an unbridgeable rift between Nottinghamshire and South Yorkshire. Before – Clifton Tom, Clarkson and Co surrounded in the Jolly Colliers by sixty Millers, slapped all over. After – Sparks flooring three Rotherham on his own outside the ground. To and fro. Back and forth, all the way up into town. The climatic scrap: Rotherham, who had gathered on the High Street at one end, scattered as Notts ran at them with bricks, bottles and metal shards from the scrap grounds near Millmoor. Several Rotherham stood – ex-steelworkers and miners spawned by Thatcher and her demon legions, what would you expect! – and an almighty ruck ensued. A Rotherham glassed with a milk bottle. An Arnold lad slashed along his arm. Blood spraying on Victorian brick walls and aspirational shop windows; an eighties splatter movie. Then there was the collateral

damage, the accidental outcome of a Saturday afternoon's sporting entertainment. Screaming housewives trapped in the Woolworth's doorway. Kids running for cover. Parents fleeing the melee, pushing their lightweight buggies along ravaged pavements. Shops shutting their doors as shoppers fled. Coppers racing to the scene justifying their overtime. Double decker busloads of passengers craning their necks for a better view. Smashed windows, cracking panes...

...fists in faces, boots in backs. Catherine wheel whacks. Helicopter impersonators.

Man down. A Notts lad smacked from behind – dazed, shocked, unexpected: A civilian walking past, thirty, in a suit, a shoe shop manager, a rage-forged slap thrown in pure indigence, recrimination and frustration. The heroic, incensed punch machine walked off into the distance, shouting and pointing.

Scum. Scum...all on ya...all on ya...SCUM...

...and just when the body count began to resemble that of a Peckinpah western, coppers arrived, air raid sirens.

Flashes of lemon, blue and silver, everyone on their toes.

No one died.

A milk crate full of smashed empties, the shards decorating the High Street like flecks of crystal snow...echoes of the screaming...

So what's happening on the pitch? I hear our beloved Chairman has gone a bit ethnic, HobNob said.

You're not kidding. It's like watching the Harlem fucking Globetrotters every Saturday, and half the fans have had enough, Bull said.

Not the most liberal fans in the world, Notts.

Nope. Never met anyone over forty who wasn't a racist underneath and they're voting with their feet. I'm surprised the Directors can't see it. Gates have dropped from 7,500 to just under 5,000 in six months. He's under real pressure. Losing a minimum of twenty-five large a week, they say. Wants rid of Judge, Hughes, and Bishop. All the decent players...

...not Bish, surely. I love Bish.

Bit rich for Ray Trew, it seems. He might have saved our black and white arses, but he's about as popular as a leper on a hot day indoors. The boys are going to turn on him before the end of next season. It all started with Keith Curle.

Keith Curle, HobNob said. What on earth possessed him to employ that dick? Hey. I heard a theory when I was in the Cedars.

What theory?

Why Chairman Trew – a multi-millionaire recruitment consultant, entrepreneur and an intelligent man, knowing that the average over-forties Notts follower is somewhat to the right of Adolf Hitler – has appointed three black managers, employs eighty percent black youngsters at the Academy and fills up the ground with black staff.

Why's that? Bull replied. He altered the rearview mirror. Traffic on the A1 was building up and he was down to forty miles per hour tops, slowing down. I have to confess, despite myself, and praying inwardly that his theory wasn't going to be racist, I found myself becoming interested in what HobNob had to say.

Demographics, Bull.

Demographics, Bull replied.

Nottingham, or so I have read, has four hundred and fifty seven different racial, religious, cultural and ethnic subdivisions. Considering the geographical variance, it's more diverse than London: Twelve percent of its population, approximately thirty thousand people come from one of these groups and the figure is rising all the time. The City has completely changed. Imagine if you will, Meadow Lane as a City.

Not a football stadium?

Nope. A City.

Okay.

This City is old. Eighty percent of its population is over forty. A good fifty percent of its population is over fifty. In the Derek Pavis stand, the average age of the spectator is approaching sixty. There are people I am told who are close to ninety regularly coming to the Lane. Only five percent are women. There are an insignificant number of teenagers, and hardly any kids coming through because they all follow the Shit From Over The Trent or worse, the plastic depositories who only exist on TV, like Man Utd and Chelsea. Everyone currently attending matches at Notts County Football Club is to all intent and purposes, white, old, and working class. Few of the august representatives of the four hundred fifty seven different racial sub-populations attend the Lane. Because of this, Notts end up competing for the same ageing, white, working class, and disgruntled Nottingham fan base as Rushcliffe Rovers and we're losing badly, all because of an accident of history…

Brian Clough, Bull said with a hint of resignation in his voice.

You got it in one. Brian Clough. When Chairman Trew usurped the gilded throne at Meadow Lane, everyone thought that he would just do the same marketing stuff everyone else does: Lower ticket prices, spend money on players, tell all the people waiting to die in the Pavis what they want to hear and hope for the massive fan base increase he feels Notts deserves. He didn't do this. I know that Chairman Trew and his glamorous assistant, Jim Rodwell, are well linked in with the University. They've been speaking to people. The *right* people. Top brains. Professors. What these ivory tower based panjandra have said is you may as well forget homogenous crowd increases because of the existence of Rushcliffe Rovers.

I can see that, Bull said.

See, County's Lincolnshire Moghul has invested ten million of his hard earned recruitment business capital in Meadow Lane, and he wants it back. His wallet is dying a slow death because of the traditionally crap Meadow Lane gates, so he takes a risk.

What risks does he take, HobNob?

This one, brother. Why not aim for the ethnics? *Why not make Notts County Nottingham's ethnic football team?* A place where the four hundred fifty seven different racial sub-populations can meet happily on a Saturday afternoon?

At least ten thousand of them. That's what the Chairman wants. That's what he needs.

Bradford City are doing it. They realised the staple consumers of the football feast are all dying off. By 2030, Notts County and Bradford City will have no fans because they'll all be dead. Unless...

You attract the ethnics, the New Britons.

My lad called me when I was in the Cedar, HobNob said. He said he recently played a football team, which was mostly Sikh. Turbans. They played in Turbans.

How is Mini-Beefy, Bull asked, by way of a diversion.

Top man. Going great guns. Seeing him next weekend.

Nice one. So why do we employ so many Afro-Caribbeans, Bull asked as the traffic began to grind to a standstill and the snow began to fall.

Because, dear brother, they've been here since the fifties and they've had a head start. They're the totems, the symbols. They all play football. By playing eight black players out of eleven, Trew is sending a message to the ethnic minorities and the recent arrivals of Nottingham's Fair City that Meadow Lane is open for business, and you are all welcome.

The three of us sat for a minute or so.

I had to confess (to myself) that I had never thought of it like this until he had mentioned Bradford City. The West Yorkshire club were being held up as a lower league multi-cultural flagship contrasted with a homogenous, bloated, white EPL fanbase. A cohort, which resembled on a smaller scale, the ancient flask-carrying cloth-capped foot soldiers of the Pavis stand.

He made sense (ignoring the fact I could see flaw after flaw in his logic). Like most conspiracy theories, there was a comforting, intuitive feel to them, a campfire glow; a luminescence swiftly destroyed with hard, boring evidence.

What about the Vice Presidents? The season ticket holders? The stayaway fans? Bull asked, without giving away anything he felt inside. They're already not happy.

HobNob leaned forward. He doesn't give a fuck. He's read his Pol Pot. The Little Yellow Book and that.

Who?

Pol Pot. Cambodia, 1975. Aftermath of the Vietnam War. Rather than re-educate the population after the Khmer Rouge takeover, rather than attempt to convince them of the rightness of the cause, he decided it would be simpler to kill them. A Year Zero approach. Much simpler. And cheaper.

It's Red, I interrupted.

What's red? HobNob replied.

Pol Pot's book.

Red?

Yes, Red.

HobNob thought about this a little. Okay, Little Red Book. Makes sense.

Bull got back on the plot after my interruption, which I immediately regretted making, feeling HobNob's gaze on the back of my neck.

So you're saying Trew is going to kill the Vice Presidents and the Season Ticket holders, he said.

Stone dead, brother. They're history. Our Chairman Pol Pot would have a completely new crowd and he's going to kill off the existing gang with the usual weaponry. High ticket prices. High priced tea and buns. Shit football. JLS on the pitch every Saturday supported by Sly and the Family Stone.

Bull laughed. That's taken out three thousand.

To save the village, we had to destroy it, HobNob said archly.

I think it's much more likely Chairman Trew is trying to reduce the wage bill, Bull said. Let's be realistic here.

On the contrary. Definitely more of the socio-cultural position, brother. It has unavoidable merit.

I'm going to take you back to Cedar Forest.

Nah. You're taking me to the match, he said. Putting his hand on his brother's shoulder, he leaned forward. I am so looking forward to going for a few pints and football at Meadow Lane. Hey, is it true there's a gang going about stabbing and robbing folk round Nottingham?

That's right, Bull said. Been two murders, three rapes and eight robberies. They think it's those cave dwellers underneath where dad used to work.

Near Eastcroft?

That's them. Coppers haven't a Scooby.

Who got deaded?

I know that one was a worker from the Jobcentre on his way back to Bridgford. He got deaded taking a short cut down the road behind the Kop. Stabbed. In the belly.

Could have been one of his unemployed customers. The Jobcentre is getting tough with the doleites nowadays.

The Sherlocks found a Big Issue underneath one of the victims. According to Radio Red, the homeless are under suspicion.

What, all of them?

Fuck off, HobNob.

Let's go to that good KFC at the top end of Newark. I'm starving…

In the distance, the sixteenth century ruins of Newark Castle had been framed by a blackening sky. Charles I was handed over to the Scots in its shadow. There had been an accident on the bypass, and progress had been slow.

What's this new chap like? HobNob asked.

Who?

The manager. The one few people have ever heard of.

Kiwomya? Bull replied

Yeh. That man.

I'll give him until October.

The traffic eased.

Instead of going back the country route, we took the A52 past Bingham and Radcliffe and into Nottingham. I had no idea of our destination. We could have been travelling anywhere. As the late winter squall circulated around the car, turning the dual carriageway into mire, the two brothers stopped talking. Bull turned on the CD player, and we listened to a CD by The Injured Birds. Eventually, we found the inner ring road and drove past the Queens Medical Centre through the underpass and down towards Ilkeston. We stopped off for petrol at a Shell garage, and Bull bought sweets, cans of drink and chocolate, which we divided like monks coming off a religious fast.

Where are we heading? HobNob asked.

Surprise. Not long now, Bull replied.

I love surprises.

Eventually, we found ourselves in Old Basford behind the tram crossing. We pulled up outside a suburban semi-detached on a row of similar suburban semi-detacheds. There was a pub, the Horse Guards, shut and boarded up, but other than that, we were in desirable territory. I looked at the pub – that would be flats before long, like the rest of them.

The Internet – no one socializes anymore.

Let's go and see Aunty Britney, Bull said getting out of the car.

Aunty Britney. Not seen her for years. Like, er, ever, HobNob said.

The three of us walked down a path next to a scrupulously maintained lawn. In the centre of the lawn was an ornamental wheelbarrow painted a mixture of red and blue. Unlike the famous Notts wheelbarrow, the wheel was solidly attached to the housing. One of the seven dwarves peeked out of the barrow in a green smock – a red nose and two big ears, the dwarf looked like a punch-drunk alcoholic. Indescribable flowers acting as the marching perimeter of the lawn struggled to bloom in the cold spring.

Bull knocked on the door, which opened almost immediately.

Britney was no more than twenty-five, and she looked more like a glamour model than an Aunty. Under no circumstances could I imagine her being an Aunty.

Tall, bottle tanned, wearing coal black strappy sandals, a gold ankle chain and a striped blue vest top with visible blue bra straps. Cut off denim shorts bisecting her midriff. Ash blonde hair lashed back tightly in a ponytail. Legs, infinite, muscular (yet slender), having no beginning and no end. Black nail polish on her hands and feet. A small tattoo on her ankle. I'd seen larger boobs, but I wouldn't have cared – I was more of a leg man, and she was European Champions League standard in the legs department. She was gorgeous and smelt like it. Lemon and eucalyptus were dominant fragrances. Her eyes, bright blue, flashed when she looked at us, welcoming, accessible, and her raspberry-lipped beam was the warmest thing I had seen all day.

Hi, guys, welcome to my humble abode, she said, a faint trace of Bristol in her accent. Tea? Coffee?

Bull declined. No, love, if I don't get back, my dinner is in the dog. This is me brother, HobNob.

She held out her hand. HobNob could scarcely look at her. He didn't look half as chirpy as he had earlier. He took her hand but looked at the carpet.

Don't by shy, you. Come on, I'll make you a coffee. Your brother can pick you up tomorrow after we've got to know each other. She turned on her heels and walked into the kitchen.

You cunt, HobNob said to his brother.

Wish I had an Aunty like this when we were growing up. Oh, and just in case…

Bull passed over a metallic sheet of pills, royal blue tablets. You'll probably need these. I know I would.

Uncertain, he trousered the pills wordlessly. Bull turned toward the door and waved to Aunty Britney who waved back cheerfully.

Look after him. I'll see you in the morning.

See you, love, she replied.

Leaving HobNob to his fate, halfway between elated and perplexed, we drove off, back toward Nottingham in the snow and the sleet.

Pirates

HobNob: "Bristol Rovers. I've always hated them cunts. Yet, to be honest, I have no idea why. They are one hundred and fifty miles away. Local pride is not at stake. Political strife – like Pompey versus the Saints, the mad docks thing – is absent. No significant Notts Face has ever been sliced up in Bristol – unlike at Swansea, violent Taff cunts. Hatred of Pirates came to Notts from nowhere as far as I can see.

I mean, there's a certain amount of logic, of natural logic, to hating the town in general. Arrogant bunch of inbred yokel carrot-crunching cunts if you ask me, but that's by-the-by: There's something horrible about Bristol and definitely something horrible about Bristol Rovers.

In December, this year, they were bottom of League Two. If they had been relegated to the Conference, I'd have been fucking delighted. Absolutely fucking thrilled. I'd have held a party, which would have woken a slumbering corpse. Bull and I started out fighting with Bristol Rovers. Years ago...there was this time..."

A Saturday afternoon
in the mid-to-late eighties:

The Horse and Groom pub. Wheeler Gate: Two pints of Ayingerbrau. I'm twenty-one, and Bull is sixteen. Bull is smartly dressed, but I can never be bothered with dressing up for the match. Weddings and court. That will do me. Don't even bother getting dressed up to take birds out.

We sink those pints, the gassy Germanic brew leaving a metallic tang that stays with us for the rest of the day. Sunny when we leave the pub. Despite Nottingham being in the grip of the Platinum Blonde's recession, there are plenty of shoppers milling about around St Peter's Church. It always seems to be busy, Nottingham.

We decide to give the Mavericks' burger a miss and walk straight down the pedestrianised precinct. We stop off at The Sawyers opposite Burtons. Used to work there. I tell Bull about the fight I saw one Saturday afternoon in 1981.

Sunderland.

Sparks, Wilconnen, Alan C and Wilman and about ten of their lot. ARA. It was a great punch-up, and I tell Bull that it was all I could do not to run out of the shop and join in. Sparks was punching the shit out of some Sunderland shadey right in front of our window. Shoppers scattering all over the place. One Sunderland fan took a right beating. When the filth finally arrived to save the Wearsiders from further punishment, one of them lay in the doorway of the opticians, not moving much, his limbs flopping at an awkward angle.

Bull tells me that he has heard me tell this tale before and we carry on, drinking our Hofmeister. We play *Defender* on the table top Space Invader game in the Sawyers. He wins – I have zero eye-hand co-ordination, and I definitely can't play Defender, except to use the Smart Bomb, but I like looking at the pretty colours and listening to the sounds, the tinny, dinking, beeping noises.

We drink up, walk through Broad Marsh and go into the King John. Two more pints of lager. The place is packed with people, none of whom is going to see Notts County.

Gates are down this season. The recession, the non-stop fighting, Forest up with the pacesetters, and the perennial lack of success at County means that people can't be arsed to visit Meadow Lane. Me? I'll always go. Bull's the same. I love County. It's family. Can't be bothered with people who pick and choose games. Can't be doing with the excuse makers. Notts have more than most. We're fucking plagued with hundreds of the cunts.

If you're County, you turn out for the match.

That's it. End of natter. That's the full SP.

Here, in the King John, they're all playing pool or chatting up birds. We drink up and head toward the Bentinck near the train station. We're buzzing. The Bentinck is my favourite pub, and we stand at the bar. Colonel George, who runs the place, knows full well that at least one of us is underage, but as long as we don't cause trouble and get in the road of the regulars, he doesn't mind. No one minds. The coppers don't care about underage drinking. They're a bit preoccupied with kicking the fuck out of miners, Socialist Workers and blacks. In Arnold, where we're from, I've been drinking since fifteen. Bull and I celebrated his sixteenth birthday in The Eagle one lunchtime, a new build smack in the middle of Killisick. After about four pints of Five Star, I accidentally let it slip to the landlord that we were celebrating his sixteenth birthday. This was in the days of last orders at two thirty, so we only had half an hour to go. He let it pass. We didn't go in there for a bit, just in case.

Colonel George serves us our Ayingerbrau, and we stand. The pub is full of travellers, bums, Forest, Meadows and Bristol Rovers and everyone mixes easily. Crammed in like sardines, and George has two staff on to deal with the crush. We move away from the bar and stand near the toilets, chattering, and when supping is done, we finish our pints, feeling fucking brilliant, and walk down toward London Road. We don't bother going through The Meadows because it's one of those really, *really* tough areas where trouble can happen on an empty street. I've had a pint or two in some pubs in the Meadows, and it is always better to go in with a local. That's a rule. A Meadows man can get shirty. A Meadows man would scar you for life for looking at his bird. Or even wearing the wrong shirt. Meadows geezers are the type of psychos who won't stop kicking you until you lie very still and dribble spills onto the pavement along with the blood.

Past the station and on to the General Gordon where we down two more pints of lager. To the Norfolk, which is full of Bristol Rovers. The pub is dirty as usual but smellier. Rovers are singing. In the corner, several County are playing pool and the Rovers fans are eyeing them up.

There is a jukebox playing, and from nowhere, the Kenny Rogers song *Coward of the County* is played.

Some Rovers fans laugh.

I see Bull tense.

Let's do these bastards, he says.

I shake my head. We don't stand a chance.

I don't care, he says. Look at that lad. He nods at a carrot-crunching Rovers fan chortling as if he had just been told the world's funniest joke. A surfer look-a-like with blonde hair down to his shoulders and a pink Lacoste tee shirt. He looks over, noticing he is being stared at by Bull, and Bull stares at him even harder. I tap my bro on the shoulder and reluctantly, in his case, we drink our pints. We leave the pub – we're not followed.

What did you do that for? He asks.

It's early, and there are loads of them, I reply. They'll kick the fuck out of us.

Rovers bastards, he says.

He's getting drunk. He's getting livid.

I had noticed this about Bull. Drink releases the rage and ideally, we should stop supping, but we soon find ourselves outside the Navigation. Bull comes out of the pub with four pints as it is getting near kick off time. It's mostly Notts outside the Navi, and there is a bustling atmosphere. Several coppers observe impassively as Rovers fans walk past unmolested, but Bull is staring at them, simmering inside. He has that killing look in his eye, the one he always gets when he's had a few pints. Not knowing anyone around us, means we keep to ourselves. Most of the people I went to school with are Forest and the County fans I do know, don't drink anything like we do.

We finish the four pints. I feel a bit pissed; don't know about Bull. There's hardly anyone walking to the ground – yet another poor gate. We walk down the Lane and toward the ramshackle Roadside where all the boys congregate, the echoing wooden stand. On a good day, the boys can make some serious noise. When we lost 5-1 at home to Villa, the din was incredible – admittedly helped by their Shadeys in the seats.

We pay our admission and take our places. Rovers have brought plenty, and they are in the bottom corner of the Kop.

Notts start to sing.

Super Notts! Super Notts!
Super Notts! Super Notts!

Glory Glory Notts County, Glory Glory Notts County

County!
County!
County!

Bull is uninterested in events on the pitch, and he's looking round for somewhere to lean. We find a spot near the side wall. He tells me he's bored already, like a big kid. Says he's thirsty. We squeeze our way past the banks of standing Notts fans – the green jackets, the shadeys, the punks, the teds, the rockers, the straights, the families, the pissed-up old geezers in stolen NCB donkeys, and women in big coats – and find ourselves in front of the serving hatch behind the stands.

I had been chatting up Karen, the young blonde who serves us pies and Bovril every week. She is no looker, but God above has blessed her with a curvy body, decent tits and a dirty looking leer. I suspect strongly that Karen would be up for every form of sexual practice known to man, and her demeanour suggests that I wouldn't be waiting long before the amusement began. I thought I was in with a chance, so I turned on the charm (as I did every week).

Just as I was about to go into overdrive, Bull tapped me on the shoulder.

Look. Rovers.

Where.

Harassing that mong.

I see them.

In front of the other hatch further down the roadside, two beefy lads in their twenties are around a Notts fan and they are giving him a hard time.

I don't know the victim's name, but you would always see him down the Lane. A shirter. Big thick spectacles and greasy Adolf Hitler hair complete with cow lick. He's the type of twat who would walk down the Kings Road in Chelsea, singing Notts songs in front of their main pub. A daft lad, the Scousers would call him. The prospect of a battering didn't bother him, apparently, or he was far too thick to see the potential.

The Rovers have him pinned back against brick. They are about to slap him.

I turn to Karen and say, see you darling, and we trot towards him, to the rescue, the beer gods commanding us.

This is what we wanted.

This is what we wanted to *be.*

And this is much more fun than the shitty football going on in the background.

The two Rovers turn toward us. Bull is bigger than one of them and the other is bigger than me. Both have longish hair like surfers. All the Rovers fans seem to have long hair, like they'd just come back from a session riding longboards at Mavericks.

The tall one advances toward me, grinning, all denim jacket and faded jeans.

He wants it, I can tell.

This knowledge makes me content. It fills me with calm. Equilibrium.

As he approaches, a sense of certainty descends that this upcoming scenario is somehow, meant to be.

There is a mutual acceptance. A tacit agreement that extreme violence is about to take place, that punches will be thrown, that blood will be spilled, and that one of us is going to be hurt, possibly quite badly.

Maybe very badly, indeed.

His concordance makes the game we are about to play seem somehow, socially acceptable, so bearing that in mind, I throw my coffee in his face, and he screams, falls to his knees. I follow up with a kick to his nose. He howls, the coffee grains scalding. I boot him in the balls. Bull headbutts the other Pirate, and he goes down with a crash. The lad with the burns is down, and before he can react, I boot him in the ribs. To the side of me, Bull is helicoptering the living shit out of the other one – his nasal plasma staining the nineteenth century bricks with inky crimson blobs.

They hadn't expected this.
They had expected to win.
They came in our end and expected easy sport.
The old Forest mantra.
The old bullies chant.
The European Cup chorus.
All the bandwagon jumping cunts.

Little County.
County's got no lads.
Little County.
Wankers, County.
Got no lads.

I think about this as I kick him again, for luck.

The melting Pirate squeals like a little girl underneath my Nike Bruins, his cheeks and nose baking in the ambient heat, flesh peeling and his skin itching as it oozed and slithered.

He must have thought like the Forest bullies at my school; otherwise, he wouldn't have come here. Into the Roadside.

The other Pirate squealing like a baby as my brother whacks him unmercifully must also have thought that, or he wouldn't have accompanied his friend here.

He should have stayed away.

I know this to be true, and I don't feel guilty at all, and I know I won't feel guilty either, at any time in my life.

They were up for it before this crushing defeat at our hands.

They came in our end.

(Yo Ho Ho)

They walked in with a Bristolian Swagger.

They laughed uproariously.

(And a Bottle of Rum)

They picked on the daftest, saddest, bloke in the building.

(Little County)

Then, they met us.

The rescued Notts in the milk-bottle lens glasses stands there oblivious to what's going on around him. I ditch the empty plastic cup and stamp on my victim one more time. I gesture to Bull. He kicks his personal Pirate in the ribs for good measure.

Keen to escape the inevitable appearance of William and his truncheon, we run up the stairs next to the Roadside seats and snake our way behind the massed ranks of spectators.

Halfway down the line, we merge into them, the ring fenced, blank faced zombie spectators, pacified and anaesthetised by the dreadful anti-spectacle unveiling before them on the emerald green turf. I turn and look to see if we were followed.

Coppers appear on the touchline, and they're with the chap I sorted out.

They're looking for us, I say.

Bull nods. Nice one with the coffee grenade, he says.

Next to us, a skinhead in a Crombie asks, you two been at it? We nod. He takes off the big black military coat and passes it to me.

Wear this and shut the fuck up, he says. Get behind me.

His mate passes Bull his green jacket. Bull puts it on and stands behind me. The coppers and Redface walk in front of us, pointing out people on the terraces. They walk slowly to where we find ourselves. His mate isn't with him. Sparked out in front of the tea stand.

My heart is beating ten to the dozen, pulsating. If he spots me, I'll be lucky to get away with a fine.

What would they charge me with?

Burning a Pirate with hot coffee.

(...pieces of eight, pieces of eight...)

ABH? GBH?

Malicious Wounding?

(Oh, bollocks.)

More like six months in Lincoln, if I find myself facing the wrong beak at the Magistrates.

(Sorry, dad.)

Hanging Judge Geoffrey.

(I didn't know I had the coffee in my hand, guv.)

Burn him.

Burn him.

The Witchfinder General.

Burn him.

Burn him.

There are the practical implications.

Bang goes my degree in History.

Bang goes a decent job.

Bang goes all my dreams,

Bang goes my father's aspirations.

Bang goes the family reputation.

I'm shitting it.

I'm wearing a Crombie, bit big for me, and there's the Pirate, tears in his eyes, his cheek shredded and crimson, boiled like a fucking lobster in a Tokyo sushi bar.

He's right in front of us on the touchline. Two big coppers on either side of him, two big ugly coppers, like that mob at Birmingham City, half copper/half bouncer, nothing like the kindly Dixon of Dock Green political stereotypes the BBC pacifies us with, his fairness, gentle admonishments and wise homilies, or the lofty, beloved copper with the handlebar moustache patrolling his beat in the Market Square.

These are modern coppers.

Psycho meatheads spawned by Henley Training Centre to combat football hooligans and striking politicals.

Post-war paramilitaries.

Thugs and beaters.

Thatcher's Praetorian Guard.

Fresh from battering the living fuck out of striking miners and their weeping wives.

There are no rules.

Fuck the Copper's Geneva Convention:
They catch me, and I'm in for a kicking.
(Sport)
They're scanning the throng of County.
Time stops still.
Red Face looks at me directly.
Our eyes meet.
Here we go.
Here we go.

The moment seems to last an hour.

He looks at me straight in the eyes.

His cheek bubbles and blisters burgundy more than red as if he had lain down for hours on his side in thirty five degree sun, on a beach in Magaluf. In August. After far too much ale.

I suppress the urge to cry and to run to the front, to tell the nice mister policemen that I'm sorry, sorry, sorry, sorry.

I don't know what came over me. The confessional tranquillity that accompanies the passing of guilt. The harmony of something *ending* twinned with the peacefulness of admission.

(Bless me father for I have sinned. This afternoon, I threw a boiling hot cup of coffee in the mush of a rival

football supporter. I smelled the flesh on his cheeks as they shrivelled...)

(Ten Hail Marys, a Sanctum Ergo and don't do it again.)

I'm lucky.

In a moment frozen in time and space, he shrugs his shoulders to the burly cops and walks toward the Rovers end. The eight hundred or so Pirates on the right hand side of the Kop are giving him a round of applause for trying to take our end, which I know will make him feel better, the scorched-faced cunt.

I shake the skinhead's hand, and he introduces himself.

I'm Jack, he says. Whisky Jack. I'm from Newark. I give him his coat back. If I were you, I'd fuck off as fast as possible. Half time. Bottom gates, out the road. You've had a winner, lad.

Bull listens to this and agrees. At half time, we keep our heads down, and head toward the end gates, tell the old soldier on the gates that we have experienced enough of that shit. He reminds us that we can't come back in.

We lie and say that we ain't *ever* coming back.

He opens the gates, and we amble toward the Meadows and take a bus back into town.

A few years later, when Bull was banned, we fought with a mob of Pirates in the alley opposite the Navigation and then (this is brilliant), on the pitch after a cup semi-final. Phil Stant had a perfectly good goal disallowed in the last minute of injury time.

To this day, sensible Notts fans say that the referee had somewhere to be that night and couldn't be arsed with the extra time because there is no way that goal should have been disallowed.

Rovers fans invaded the pitch.

So did we.

A mad battle in the centre circle ensued. I cracked two of them, one a beauty on his cheek, and then, I got a slapping myself. It was a bit like one of those old seventies films with the flares and the long hair and the platform soles going in, sticking the boot in and for some reason, it all happened in slow motion.

Clifton Tom saved my bacon that day. The coppers were coming for me, and I needed an arrest like a hole in the head, but he stopped one of them who had me in his sights and distracted him by pointing out more Rovers attempting to get onto the pitch, and the copper attended to that while I merged into the demented stands. Bull was banned that year for that shit up at Chesterfield.

We've fought with Rovers at Toddington Services outside their main pub in Bath, outside that newsagent at Twerton Park and behind the Roadside after Caskey skanked them with the ungentlemanly throw in that he should never have taken.

We hate them…but it's been fun knowing them…

3. Cicero

We picked him up first thing in the morning. Sitting on the wall outside Aunty Britney's semi-detached. When he got into the car, I felt a draught invade the heated interior, a sprite summoned by the eternal British winter. HobNob didn't seem to notice the cold and he sat in the back, in the middle, equispaced, hands on his knees.

I looked at his eyes in the rearview mirror. Puddle grey semi-circles orbited eyeballs of ebony. He needed a shave. Despite being in Cedar Forest for an age, he was stocky, bordering on overweight.

I was thinking last night, he said. Do you think it was a good idea to get rid of Curle this late in the season? I sometimes think that Chairman Trew is a bit nippy on the trigger.

Bull looked at me, incredulous. Then he turned to his brother.

Is that all you have to say?

What do you mean?

You know.

What?

Come on… how was the delightful Aunty Britney?

HobNob looked out of the window nonchalantly. She was alright, he said.

Alright, brother? She cost me a wedge.

Yeh, she was nice, he said, distant, as if he was engaging in a particularly uninteresting conversation about lawnmowers. She's a Red, and it put me off a bit. I was shagging her and she started talking about Billy Davies, which was something of a passion killer. Why is it that people who move to Nottingham always end up following Forest?

I didn't check her affiliations with the agency. I AM sorry. I'll do better next time, Bull said. Anyway, I think the opposite.

What?

Lots of people who move to Nottingham end up following Notts, he postulated.

That's not my experience, he replied, leaning forward, looking in the rearview mirror and stiffening the remnants of his black hair into spikes with both hands. About Keith Curle, he continued. I tried to discuss the situation with her last night, but she had no idea who I was talking about.

Curle had to go, Bull said. He was costing us five hundred fans a week. Any more Keith Curle football and there would be you, me, scribbler here, Haxford, Clifton Tom and Chairman Trew's fanatic missus Aileen watching from the Pavis. Plus, all the oldies.

Plus, all the oldies, HobNob parroted, ironically. That lot will be competing to be the last one to turn out the lights.

Most of them can remember Lawton, I joined in.

Lawton, HobNob replied. He who used to hover in the air like a falcon about to swoop on a dormouse in the corn. The Raptor. Tommy Lawton: The man that defied the laws of physics. Lawtonman. *Hoverman*...

They've been waiting for the new Lawton ever since, Bull commented.

Tony Hateley came close, I said. And Sir Lesley Bradd.

Nah, HobNob observed. They could head a ball, but they couldn't *hover* in the air. Remember what dad said?

I can, yes. Lawton used to float, then crane his neck and like a ricochet, he'd plant it in the top corner. There wasn't a centre back who could cope with him. I'm taking you round to your new digs. You're expected.

Where am I staying?

Lodgings. I've paid three months in advance. You can pay me back when you get a job.

Cheers, he said. Thanks for doing all this, Bull.

I'm waiting for my pocket money. You said you'd give me pocket money when we were growing up.

HobNob sat back, the slightest grin. I looked at him in the rearview mirror. It was difficult to tell what he was thinking. Whether he was happy. Whether he was pissed off. I had heard many things about HobNob. I had heard he used to be a teacher – the most common rumour about him – but every time I asked anyone, no one knew.

Or if they did, they weren't prepared to share.

Bull did something with power stations along the East Coast and in far-flung Kipling countries like Azerbaijan, and he made a pretty pile out of it, but he was much more open than HobNob. All I knew about him was that he spent an awful lot of time unemployed. Bull had told me earlier. It stood to reason. It would have been a rare employer to keep a job open after an eight-month hiatus, and as I knew – as he had *admitted* – his many criminal records acquired for football violence over the years would have automatically barred him from the sort of jobs that *would* wait for him for eight months.

Like teaching.

He was smart and clever (except when drunk) and could have taken many, many jobs, but it was clear careers hadn't interested him. I didn't know what interested him, approaching fifty. What were his plans? I made a note to ask him, but while he and Bull would talk all day about, say, battering a van load of Shrewsbury at Watford Gap services, getting anything out of them regarding reality was like chopping down an oak tree with a kitchen knife.

They just weren't interested. It just didn't bother them.

The only thing outside football they had ever seemed to talk about was horse and greyhound racing.

We pulled into the McDonald's drive-in in Basford and without asking, Bull ordered three breakfasts, plus three bacon and egg McMuffin's, three orange juices and three coffees. I certainly couldn't argue with his choice, but I would struggle to eat the bacon and egg on top of the breakfast. One of the brothers, no doubt, would help me out. The coffee and orange juice would be much appreciated.

Before long, we were sitting outside the new lodgings on the border between Aspley and Wollaton, munching, listening to the radio and watching random flakes of snow swirl in the wind.

We're a bit early, Bull said. I'll text her to let her know we're here.

He did so. The lodging house had a plaque outside, and as I tucked into one of the McMuffins, I strained to see the writing. It looked like **Cicero's**, named after the Roman poet. I did a double take.

Yes, Cicero's.

Whether Hobnob approved of the lodgings or not – a standard three bedroom semi-detached, front lawn, back lawn, paved garage, suburban to the core – he didn't say. Nor did he ask how Bull had located the lodgings, whether it was someone he knew, whether it was a regular lodging house he sourced from a directory, or the internet, or whether this was a favour from a friend. He seemed to be shrugging his shoulders, taking whatever his brother sorted for him with equanimity and a lack of engagement. To me, HobNob seemed to lack gratitude – his thank you earlier lacking sincerity – but maybe it was just reticence and social awkwardness. It could also have been guilt or embarrassment. Maybe he was always like this, but when I met him last year, he was a lot more animated, almost controlling, like a leader, like someone who wanted the command of the ship. Like someone who *needed* command.

Thinking this, I felt guilty – he'd been in the Cedar Forest for eight months, since the end of last season. That was bound to have had some impact on the emotions.

The Cedar Forest.

Last night, while Aunty Britney entertained HobNob and Bull did whatever he does in the evenings, I sat down in my flat, cracked open a four pack of Thor's Hammer and spent three hours searching on the Internet for information on Cedar Forest.

All I knew was that HobNob had been sent there after the last match of the season in 2012 versus Brighton. No one would say why, and I suspect even if they knew, they wouldn't tell me. I don't know who sent him there – or whether he went there voluntarily. I don't know whether it was a legal or family issue. All I know is that he was incarcerated. He could not leave – Bull intimated that much. The coppers could have had everything to do with his stay or nothing to do with it. It could have been rehab. Family led. A resort, a prison, a hospital, a health lodge or a mental asylum.

Bull was saying nothing and I was curious enough to ask him, but I was also inquiring enough to do my own research and put the pieces of the jigsaw puzzle together.

It proved to be a frustrating task.

I tried everything I knew, every protocol, every combination of words, the lot.

And I know my way around a PC, believe me.

I drew a blank.

I tried search engines apart from Google, and I could not find a single comment about Cedar Forest. I found several Googleblogs, which purported to be from ex-residents, but they were all disused. Voidblogs. Drivebys. I went through the archives of each. One had been wiped clean, which struck me as suspicious. I found Cedar Lodge on a disused NHS service directory, but with no phone number or e-mail address. That wouldn't have been unusual. Lots of organisations work with the NHS. Other than that, there was nothing. Not a comment. Not a website. Not a phone number. Not a review. Not a word. No snide comments on a discussion group, no observations on a net seminar. Nothing on Facebook and Twitter. Nothing on there at all. I tried academic search engines ("The Professor"). I tried paralegal protocols, probation documentation. I searched the alleys, warrens and ginnels of academic psychology to discover whether HobNob had been staying in an asylum, but that proved less than fruitless, if that were possible.

I found what I am about to say hard to believe, but I found it to be true – it appeared that Cedar Forest did not exist on the Internet.

You might consider that an impossibility in the modern world.

Go on. Try it.

Prove me wrong.

Maybe the place had never existed. You can find page after page from the early days of the net, old dot-net stuff, old newsgroups, bulletin boards, but my search couldn't confirm categorically whether Cedar Forest *had ever* existed on the Net. I tried Direct.gov. I tried the Prison Service. I tried the Home Office. I even called a couple of serious geeks I know and asked them to help me. They could find no trace of the place I visited yesterday and saw with my own eyes. And these guys can find a missing full stop in a million line Java program.

It vexed me.

We passed all the breakfast detritus to Bull, and he put it all in a Tesco carrier bag, got out of the car and put the whole lot in the boot. Then, he popped his head back inside.

She's here, look, Bull said. Mrs Queen.

I looked up the pathway to the house. A woman in her fifties with magenta coloured hair, permed, over her shoulders, a cobalt blue sweatshirt and baggy jeans, stood at her door. She smoked a cigarette. Hoop earrings dangled like miniature dustbin lids from her ears, and she seemed to be watching us.

You stay here, Bull said to me. I'll get HobNob settled. Come on...

HobNob scrambled from the car, picked up his rucsac, and followed his brother up the driveway. I had no idea why I hadn't been allowed inside and part of me, the writer part, was disappointed, and because of that, I guess I was as passive as HobNob was in my own way.

I could have argued. I didn't.

The three of them disappeared into the suburban house, Cicero's doorway swallowing them up completely as if they had never been there.

Brentford Away Part I

Bull: *"After the Brentford lads had travelled up to pay us a visit that afternoon, it was imperative, nay, urgent – that the Notts crew travel down to Griffin Park to return the compliment. It was so nice to see them that day. It was like having a visit from relatives. Coffee and cake. A sneaky crème de menthe, The Generation Game with Bruce Forsyth on the telly. It would be rude for us not to return the favour..."*

A Saturday afternoon
in the late nineteen eighties…

…discussed the plan on the terraces in the weeks leading up to the away fixture in West London. Decided that a transit van would be the appropriate method of transport. A plain white van: Cheap, anonymous and the ultimate Trojan horse.

The standard hooligan method of delivery.

The Galaxy C5 of fighting boys transport.

What it lacked in comfort, it made up for in camaraderie, and the journey to Brentford would be no more than two hours, given a sunny day and decent weekend traffic.

It made sense.

Whatever Thatcher was doing to the North continued, and money was tight. Besides, the lads were bound to be thirsty and eager to guzzle in the quartet of pubs surrounding Griffin Park, one on each corner. That would be money well spent. Countless hooligan gangs travelled the length of the country every Saturday in transit vans; inexpensive all-purpose builder vehicles with no seating, just planking. Twenty people in the back, which meant that away travel could be just as cheap as going to a home match, and there would be more money for beer.

Cardiff's Soul Crew, Burnley's Suicide Squad and Millwall's Bushwhackers were three gangs who made good use of the transit to carry out their raids around the country. Vans were useful tools: Not only were they cheap, but they were inconspicuous. Cars required co-ordination and planning. Coppers could lockdown a mainline train station full of Leicester in fifteen minutes flat and would happily pull over a coachful of lads on their way to Stockport, and proceed to spoil their day with escorts and no-drinking orders.

However, coppers would need the word of a grass to prevent a transit trundling along on the motorway.

White van man.

White van hooligan.

How could the coppers tell without inside info? Especially if the transit travelled first thing in the morning or better, as with the extreme Northern firms (Carlisle, for example), or the extreme Southern gangs (Plymouth, Portsmouth), travelling overnight, arriving somewhere tasty just in time for breakfast.

In total, at various matches before the March trip, twenty two handpicked men confirmed their availability for a day out in London. Sparks, who had organised it, knew that some would drop out at the last minute, so that was fair enough. Sixteen in the back, seven on each side and two at the ends. Three up front including the driver. Sparks, older than the rest of them, booked the transit van from standard sources. A pipe fitter by trade, he was used to booking this kind of stuff, and he got a fat discount.

The lads, including the Bully brothers, were all from Arnold, a suburb four miles north of Nottingham City Centre. Mostly remnants of the Arnold Republican Army, an offshoot hooligan gang that generally hung around Arnold Town Football Club.

The inclusion of HobNob in the firm had been a matter of debate. He had a history with Sparks and some of the other lads, which went back to school days. Details were hazy. Talk of a fight. HobNob mixing with a different crowd. Another nasty brawl one night in Daybrook. Another, a riot after a school disco at the catholic school HobNob attended. The wrong person beaten up in a street, an innocent victim, collateral damage. Because of all that, HobNob was an ARA target for about a year before someone pointed out how stupid regional fighting was and someone else pointed out to Sparks that HobNob was Notts, and suddenly, the hierarchical rules kicked into play.

Football was more important.

While HobNob was not forgiven – there were three people on the transit trip to Brentford who would have cut him the first chance they got – Sparks was highly respected, the King of the Jungle, and if he said that the *fatwa* on HobNob was lifted, then it was so.

Bull was exempt from the war politics. Nineteen to HobNob's twenty four; he missed all the school high jinks, all the regional jibba jabba. He was clean. Tabula rasa. His brother had allied himself with a massive gang on the other side of Arnold, and it was remembered.

It could be recalled.

He had clashed in the past with at least six of the travellers on the trip to Brentford, and given the wrong set of circumstances, things might get edgy, and in the uncomfortable planked confines of a transit the size of a paddy wagon (plus the speed, booze, fags, dope and the memories), very violent indeed.

Bull could have been anyone. They were pleased to see him. For better or for worse, everyone on the transit trip knew him solely as HobNob's younger brother and in his own right, one of the most pathologically violent football hooligans ever seen at Meadow Lane. Certainly, up there in the rankings, a First Division rogues gallery you wouldn't want to write to your grandmother about.

Sparks.

The Mad Postman.

Whisky Jack.

Some of Haxford's men.

Staffy.

Big Pridge.

A few of the older lads who mixed with Forest sometimes (which pissed Sparks off no end).

People like Paddy Blackland, Paul Wilconnen, Dean Wilman and Alan Crenshaw, an ARA vet who also mixed it with Leeds and Millwall, anywhere he could find a punch-up.

Some older skinheads who didn't travel away much (but who nevertheless, you wouldn't want to meet in the street after dark).

The Bully brothers.

When Sparks asked them whether they wanted to come down to London on the OHT (the Official Hooligan Transit as he called it), the two brothers agreed, but then went to the pub alone and discussed the situation.

Bull knew that HobNob was a marked man around one side of Arnold and that several people on the transit were likely to be part of the *fatwa*. They discussed it. They knew that Sparks, the top man at Meadow Lane and highly respected, had made his papal bull to the masses, and that, in a sense, was a guarantee that nothing *tragic* would occur. At least, that's what the two of them chose to believe, and because of that, they decided to make the trip, that Saturday afternoon in March.

Eighteen turned up. The Bully brothers met the OHT at the Broxtowe Inn on the exit road to the M1. HobNob wore a flesh pink Ocean Pacific sweatshirt with an impermeable beer stain on the front, like a faded Rorschach test. His wedge haircut made him look a little like Shaun Ryder of the Happy Mondays. Ill-fitting ripped jeans and battered Nike Bruin trainers completed the repellent impression.

Bull, by contrast, was dressed in a decent new Harrington style dark blue bomber, jeans and Adidas Forest Hills. He had showered and enjoyed an early night. Bull didn't always dress up, but this was an occasion to do exactly that. Remembering that Brentford had dressed up to the nines with Tacchini tops and Aquascutum jeans and Lacoste polo shirts, he didn't want to let the side down.

His brother couldn't give a fuck. A night spent drinking with the Skull in town ending in Camelots, with two giant breasted slappers from Bilborough who ended up shagging a couple of weird Goths because both football lads were off their heads and the Skull, as was his wont, had fallen asleep in a corner as the DJ played *Tainted Love* by Soft Cell, a ditty the Camelots' DJ was very fond of indeed.

As a result, HobNob's eyes were bloodshot and underscored with concentric charcoal ripples that made him look like a vampire panda.

Smoking non-stop on the car park, he crushed his final one when the transit came to a halt in front of him, Sparks driving.

HobNob was nervous (he didn't say anything to his brother).

They went round the back and opened the white van doors, took a position.

No one in there smiled.

No one moved.

No one greeted the men.

The atmosphere went from chilly to Arctic in seconds.

The Bully brothers froze.

Sean Church pulled out a decorator's knife and showed it to HobNob.

Up for it today, son? He asked.

Compact, black haired, chunky and violent, like many of them in the back of the transit, he wore a coat and boots combo as if he were going for a day's shark fishing off Perranporth beach. The glint in his eye seemed to reflect off the blade; three inches long, new, the blade sharp enough to gouge flaps from skin.

Everyone in the van stared at HobNob.

Church rotated the decorator's knife in his hand, and his expression was indecipherable.

Then, Sparks turned round.

You're such a scruffy cunt, HobNob

...and everyone took that as their cue for the laughter to begin.

HobNob and Bull joined in, relieved to high heaven, and Sparks pulled out onto the slip road, merged into the motorway bound traffic.

Out came the fags.

Out came the beer.

It was a day out in London after all.

The journey down didn't take long, and within two hours, the van pulled up in a free parking space outside a garage on the main Brentford High Street.

Sunny and serene, with none of the hubbub you generally witnessed in the streets around other grounds.

They were all happy to arrive. It was cramped in the back and legs needed to stretch.

Sparks turned round to address the troops.

It's only twelve so let's take it easy. Remember. Them Brentford were incognito on their day out up to the Lane, and we want to do them in their ground. Return the compliment. In their end. No scrapping in pubs or outside Allied Carpets, gentlemen. We want to do those cunts right in their own living room. We'll split up and meet up about ten to three. The away seats are right above their main boys. That's where we're going. Alright? I'll see you there. I'm going for a McDonalds, he said. See you bastards in a bit.

The back doors opened, and everyone disembarked.

Bull gestured to HobNob, and the two of them went their own way. No matter who they travelled down with, they did their own thing, found their own pubs, enjoyed the freedom and the space. They sometimes found a bookies and bet on Hackney Dogs. They always got a burger down their necks. On one famous night (in the Bully pantheon, that is), the two of them drove to Southampton: The Dell, Alan Shearer number nine, and before they went to the match, they spent twenty eight quid at the Burger King on the precinct.

Two whoppers, two whoppers with cheese, two bacon double cheeseburgers, thirty chicken nuggets, eight bags of onion rings and endless boxes of fries, topped off with four apple and blackcurrant pies and washed down with four large Sprites.

They ordered all this in homage to Larry Fishburne in *King of New York*.

Only rather than being arrested by hard-core NYPD detectives before they could eat a morsel, they ate to their heart's content...

...drank themselves insensible over the course of the next three hours. At least ten pints. Brentford FC famously, has four pubs on each corner of the ground, and the two of them drank in all four. In one, they met up with Haxford, Breaker, Clifton Tom, Little Dave and the Printer, who were guzzling contentedly. The brothers chatted to them about anything but football, and they revealed their plans. Common knowledge that there was going to be a little of the old Tit-For-Tat going on.

They came in our seats...we'll go in theirs.

Clifton Tom said he was considering joining in, but he was more of a drinker nowadays, content to sup his fill, only hitting people as a last resort. Notts were a big drinking firm – latterly emptying the barrels at the Pack Horse outside Bury by two o'clock one Saturday afternoon, leaving the landlord sending out for new supplies, a feat only ever matched by Bristol City.

Haxford was the same. Mild mannered and magnanimous, except with coppers and stewards. Here was a bloke who had to be in charge. It was his nature, his essence, and the sight of a gobby fat geezer in a yellow vest ordering him about, was like a red flag to a bull. Countless times, Haxford found himself on his coach having a kip with the match he'd travelled hundreds of miles to see not twenty minutes gone.

Haxford had used trains and cars to see his beloved Notts with his crew, but he had lately started organising coach trips and so far, the police had allowed his tours to go as close to the ground as they wanted: He wasn't expecting this state of affairs to last much longer. He was telling the brothers that some forces were ambushing coaches and vans twenty miles away from the stadia and following them in with bike escorts, keeping the tourists out of the way in designated pubs. Other forces were asking the trip organisers to ring up in advance to inform them of their plans. Those coppers had been known to impound vehicles that didn't. This was all a legacy of thirteen years of serious violence, but most of all, it was a legacy of Luton, of Heysel, of St Andrews and of Hillsborough. Demoness Thatcher had cried enough, and the coppers were getting as tough with hooligans as they had done with the miners. Some matchdays resembled Eastern European Police States: Evil faced coppers everywhere, sirens blaring, lines upon lines of constables, phalanxes of horses like helmeted sunflower coloured Dragoons ready to charge football followers in trainers and pit jackets and women in big coats (a constituency nearly extinct).

Naturally, gates had dropped badly.

Brentford weren't expecting more than four thousand to today's match, and in London, that was a catastrophic number, and despite the potential for trouble, the Four Landlords of the Brentford Apocalypse, one on each corner, weren't turning away any Notts fans. Everyone's money was good with only four thousand expected and a small percentage boozing.

Keeping a watchful eye on things as they drank, scanning the streets for any sign of the Brentford lads who had raided Meadow Lane, the Bully brothers downed pint after pint and then they started on the vodka. A Viking trick. Fill the warriors full of as much booze as they can handle, point them in the direction of the enemy (some village, some cohort of English peasantry), and then let them loose.

Disinhibited. Dislocated from reality. Blind Fury. Berserker wrath.

Bull was getting more and more into it, the more beer went down. He was a seriously angry man when he'd had a pint, a man likely to pull the world into his rage, like hapless stars being dragged into the gravitational influence of a black hole in space. It was noticeable that Haxford and Clifton Tom had made their excuses, headed to the ground, leaving HobNob to keep an eye on him.

HobNob.

His elder brother.

Simultaneously, the fuse and the snuff cloth.

The more beer Bull drank (Stellas, Holstens, Snakebites, Diamond Whites. Special Brews and a new fangled German invention by the name of Becks – lethal, truly lethal), the less he laughed, the less he spoke. His eyes focusing on some non-specific point in the distance, the third eye, like a veteran of a traumatic war. Like a tracking station looking out to sea, he would start to scan for the enemy. To mutter and grunt, exhort his brother to attack any number of away fans. HobNob would try and calm him down, try to talk sense into him, which wouldn't work.

He would then pick on his brother.

Call him a coward, a cunt, a weakling. Unstoppable, he would go off on his own and attack people, unable to contain the red hot alcohol released frenzy inside him and the next time his brother would see him, as at Shewsbury on a bank holiday Monday, he would be in the midst of six burly coppers being dragged along the ground toward the hopeless jaws of a waiting Black Maria.

The brothers didn't leave the pub until ten past three. As such, they missed their appointment with the Arnold lads. One extra pint and a double vodka. The streets quiet, all a blur. Chameleons.

Naturally, the two brothers went in the home end, Bull paying for the tickets using his best cockney accent.

The duo stood at the bottom of the stairway, which led up to the Brentford terraces. The sound of exhortation could be heard all around. The sky blue and the clouds sparse. HobNob could see panoramic heavens, cobalt, never ending, in the epicentre of the keyhole at the top of the stairs, corniced by gloomy wooden stands. Bull stared at the floor, psyching himself up. Up ten terraced stairs was the home end. Their lads nearest the away following as you would expect.

Several supporters passed behind them, chattering away in west London accents.

The two of them drunk, swaying and actively shitting themselves, had three options available to them, assuming they hadn't been spotted and were about to be jumped, stabbed in the toilets and left hacked up on the walkway, the victorious assailants dispersing into the crowds.

Option One: Find a friendly looking copper and ask to be escorted to the away end. Tell him that there had been a big mistake. Appeal to his better nature with a likely sounding tale.

A mischievous Brentford fan told us this was the away end, officer. The scamp! Can you walk us round to our end, to our friends? After all, we'll be in big trouble if we stay here, won't we. There might be trouble.

With elfin smiling welcoming faces.

Option Two: Leave the same way they came in, go back to the pub and wait for it all to blow over.

Option Three: Grow a pair of concrete bollocks, run up the stairs and give it LARGE!

County!
County!
County!

And in the end, there was only one choice the Bully brothers could make.

They looked at each other.
Trotted up the top of the stairs, Bull leading.
When they reached the top, standing over the massed ranks of Brentford fans – men, women, children, shirters, pub boys, families together, wide boys in patent shoes, corpulent whisky men in Sweeney quilted car coats; besovereigned car dealers, the pride of West London – the match playing out on lush green turf, the Notts fans, a good eight hundred on the Kop to the right – they didn't have time to plan because the lad who led the charge behind the stand at Meadow Lane, Blondie, spotted them, and there were twenty of his boys with him.

There was no time to run, and only one thing to do.

With the top terrace gangway clear, the Bully brothers charged, taking the fight to them, no choice, and in the maelstrom, in the collision, the two of them found themselves surrounded.

They began to helicopter, hitting everyone they could and in return, they got helicoptered back. In the seats overlooking the terracing, Sparks and the gang took the charge as their cue, raced down to the front and started swinging punches and leaning over, stamping on Brentford heads. Somehow Breaker was in there, too, in the melee. The noise was intense, the noise of collision, of fists hitting cheekbones. Of boots connecting with skulls. Of the winding necks of cockney locals on banked terraces turning round to see who was taking the piss. Ergo, the whole stadium turned their collective gaze away from the pitch to look at the melee.

Even the Brentford fullback was momentarily distracted, the locals shrieking …

…kill the cunts, wankers, hooligans, batter the cunts, hooligans, spoiling it, hit the cunts, batter them KILL THEM…

…HobNob clouted five times before he got a proper whack in. Even that was a limp wristed air waft, a drunken slap on the bristly cheek of a long haired lad in a lilac Tacchini tracksuit top. He pulled himself together and began to hit out.

To helicopter.

Next to him in the clash, in the centre of the spin dryer (the turbulence, the track suited and be-trainered melee, the Saturday afternoon entertainment, the impromptu gladiatorial battle in the Brentford Coliseum), Bull was bleeding. The result of a Glasgow Kiss, but he stood, booted some barking random in the chest, a kung fu kick.

HobNob recovered, butted a kid in a plain white tee shirt, lashed out at an older lad in a pink Ellesse tennis shirt, connecting with the top of his leg.

In the manner of things, others ran up from the lower terracing and joined in.

Older blokes, pub men, mechanics, hard geezers, six pints after their overtime Saturday morning, workers on a black'un in their overalls. The Bully brothers in a spin dryer next to a stanchion, taking an almighty beating – fists and boots and screams and shouts, and slaps and kicks and nuts – and only the ARA above were stopping a massacre from taking place.

Before the beating approached manslaughter proportions, four yellow-coated coppers raced up from behind the stands and the Brentford mob parted like the Red Sea. The coppers grabbed Bull, the big bullseye, the easy target, gore pouring from his nostrils, a tooth loose, his nose bent and both eye sockets on the point of closing. He didn't make much of a fuss and allowed himself to be dragged away.

Before the coppers could get to him, two big Brentford dragged HobNob by his hair before the coppers knew what was happening and the momentum propelled him down the terraces.

From their positions on each levered terrace step, civilian onlookers decided it was their time to participate.

One-by-one, they kicked him on his legs as he passed, punched him on his back, up and down his arms, in the back of his head. Like something biblical, the criminal carrying a crucifix up the hill to Calvary, the people watching along the path granted their moral admonishments.

The merciful called him a cunt or a wanker, sometimes both.

Cunt. Wanker. Cunt. Wanker.

The word Northern occasionally prefixed the abusive terminology.

Greedily, some of them hit him *and* swore at him.

The people striking HobNob in slow motion weren't the hooligan bogeymen of the Sunday Mirror or the News of the World.

Skinheaded folk devils.

Red eyed harbingers of moral panic.

Uncontrollable bravos of the new nihilism.

Crazed teenagers ruined by the secularisation of society, the inability of mad scientists to prove the existence of Hell and the banning of corporal punishment.

The people hitting HobNob were civilians.

Family men.

Bearded men in donkey jackets with the incongruous and pointless shoulder patch.

Old men in caps reading programmes.

Newsagents. Bookmakers. Accountants.

Wrinkled Professors of Modern History.

Burn him!
Let him die!
Criminal!

They all had their say as he was flung headlong down the terrace.

Burger van vendors. Cigarettemakers and Butchers. Writers. Warehousemen. Newsagents. Bus drivers. Grizzled coach drivers in double breasted burgundy coach driving jackets from John Colliers, bellies the size of hot air balloons, blotchy faces, and colossal spectacles tinged copper with the tobacco smoke from sixty fags a day. Old ladies with imperial purple shopping bags made of Hessian net. Baggage men from nearby Heathrow. Stockbrokers from Threadneedle Street, with Port noses and immaculate teeth.

All of them.

They all hit him.

An equal opportunity beating.

They all went into him, his own personal spin dryer.

Pipefitters, Plasterers. Plumbers. Punks, Post-Punks, Postmen, Postmen Punks, Post-Punk Postmen, Poker Players, Pearpickers, Playboys, Pinstripes, Parkkeepers, Paedophiles, Pubmen, Priests, Pastors and Parsons.

All of them had a kick, a punch, a slap, or a swear.

The whole of London it seemed were having their say about hooligans.

Fucking hooligan. Lock him up. Ruining the game. Not in my day! Thatcher's children. Lock him up and throw away the key. What's the world coming to?

What's it going to be then, hey?

Ban them,

Burn them.

Burn the hooligan!

BURN HIM.

BURN HIM.

HobNob, bruised, his sweatshirt bloody and torn, spaced out, disoriented, took his infinite beating with commendable stoicism, the lunchtime booze numbing the pain and endorphins flooding through his system, like a good fuck, the best fuck, the adrenalin defending, not feeling it, zero state, a whiteness, a block of ice in the brain.

HobNob finally reached the bottom of the terrace, coming to a halt on pitch side.

The Notts fans on the Kop cheered and were trying to scale the fences like excited baboons in the zoo, chest beating...

County aggro, County aggro, County aggro, BULLY BULLY, oooh, BULLY BULLY, oooh BULLY BULLY

...the coppers racing round the pitch in a line...

...the yellow-coated Keystone Cops *(hello, hello, hello, what have we 'ere then)*, the carnage, the *carnage*...

...a man in a denim jacket who looked a bit like Jeff Randall in *Randall and Hopkirk,* with the same seventies mop top hair, the same flared bell bottom school trousers and shiny brown winkle pickers, his cheery phizog bisected neatly by an exotic rainforest caterpillar moustache, said alright mate, picked HobNob off the floor, ready to dust him down, a kindly soul, and with the Midlander dazed, reasonably replying, yeh, fine mate...

...Jeff Randall clouted him one, a beauty, a proper punch, a *man's* punch with knuckles, rings and due diligence, meaty, marbled *forbearance* behind the punch, a precision whack, which was done *on purpose,* which knocked him over the wall, straight into the arms of two burly coppers who smelt of shoe polish and Brut aftershave...

...one of who said, you're out, you pathetic northern knob, and the next thing he knew, he was back outside the gates of the West Stand sitting next to Bull, both of them bleeding and bruised...

4. Boring End-of-Season Match 2013

...better off in Stalag 17, HobNob said, taking a sip of his Bovril.

Should have been there with you, Bull added.

Me, too, I concluded, half way through the second half of a miserable contest at the Meadow Lane stadium.

A tedious affair at the end of a season on its last legs, the match had nothing to offer for the £24 Chairman Trew was asking. There had been no discounts, no group deals, and no buy-one-get-one-free specials for these meaningless time fillers. It was dreadful stuff. People all around us in the Pavis were expressing their disapproval. Not a single player on the pitch was worth watching on either side. All mentally on the beach in Playa already.

Yet Notts were in the lead.

Notts may have been winning, but it was a dire match. Relegation threatened Colchester. Winning can be an illusion. It doesn't satisfy or enthuse. This was one of those contests. I have seen football matches where we have lost heavily (doomed Macclesfield at home, for example, thrashing us by five or six on a freezing Tuesday night in January), and have gone home with a contented smile, but this game was only pleasing to the most jaundiced eye. Only the most fanatic win at all costs advocate would be satisfied.

I'm glad Mini-Beefy isn't here to see this, HobNob said.

He's seen a lot worse. He survived Gudjon and Charlie. And we're winning.

It's boring. We can't string two passes together.

They're worse.

It's all relative. Einstein was right. How long did you say Kiwomya's got?

October.

He won't make the end of the season at this rate. This is dreadful. Even Bish looks bored with proceedings. If Colchester weren't so bad, we'd...

Nothing to play for, I said.

And it was true.

Thoughts of play offs and even the nail biting exhilaration of a relegation struggle had passed by. With six or seven matches to go, it had been a question of getting the season over with, an expensive pastime only for the most loyal. I looked around the stadium – there were nowhere near 5,000 present: A long way short of Chairman Trew's oft-quoted business plan. A long winter dragging on into a cold spring meant everyone wore warm coats. Bull wore his Beanie, and I wore my hood up. This was April. It seemed the climate at a best guess, was a month to two months off kilter. I had read the Earth was technically in an ice age and today, it certainly felt like it. The mass burning of the rain forests in Indonesia – the wastage of the trees, the murder of countless species, the released carbon rising into the ozone layer, the uncontrollable smog shutting down the sky in the Pacific – created a similar impact on Europe to the eruption of Krakatoa.

I had some good news this week, Bull, HobNob said.

What's that?

Got a job interview.

Nice one. What for?

Oh, my old job. You know, he replied, clearly mindful of my presence and vague to the point of rudeness. Bull didn't even try to illuminate. This aspect of them irritated me to distraction.

Whereabouts, Bull replied.

Notts. Town Centre. Interview's on Wednesday.

Prospects?

If I can avoid mentioning the Cedar and can get them to believe I have been working away in the deep South, then it could be a good one.

Who's refereeing you?

My old boss…e-mailed her last night. She's always happy to help. She's a good kid, and she doesn't…

…know you were away for a bit, I know. Do you need anything from me?

Nah. Got a whistle, some nice shoes. I'll be fine.

HobNob didn't look too bad. Certainly better than last year. I remembered Hobnob from when I was interviewing him for *Ultra Violence*. He looked terrible, truly terrible. Skin as translucent as wallpaper paste. Bad teeth and profound shadowy bags that oozed down along his cheeks all the way to his top lip. At times, he looked as if he was about to die. Fags. Large quantities of booze, fast food and prescription drugs. More fags.

Today, however, he looked comparatively fresh. There was colour in his cheeks, and his spikes stood to attention. His blue eyes were on their way back to recovery, and the overwrought circles were a quarter of the size. He had lost weight – though not by much. The modern world, I knew well from one of my recent articles, saw fat people as pariahs and their suffering as self-inflicted and, therefore, deserved. Like the undeserving poor, fat people had become a scapegoat, blameworthy, an opportunity for a middle class judgement call. Taboo territory. Middle-aged men like him couldn't afford to put weight on – they would have little chance of vanquishing a younger, leaner candidate in an interview. I had spoken to a few of my friends, and all of them said the same thing. Obesity was the new smoking. The new drink driving. While HobNob wasn't obese by any means, I felt he ought to be aware. I wasn't going to say anything for obvious reasons...

(Calling me a fat bastard?)

I'll have my fingers crossed, he said. Could do with a stroke of luck. It would be nice.

Arquin skied a sitter over the bar.

It would have been easier to score. A passing cormorant found itself temporarily crushed between the football and the overhanging roof protecting the spectators in the Meadow Lane Family Stand. The shot lacked power and enthusiasm, and because of this, the cormorant was able to get up and fly away back to the Trent. To jeers, the hapless striker trotted back to the halfway line. Bishop, who had laid on the pass, watched on nonplussed in the centre circle, hands on hips. Judge gestured to the touchline, an enigmatic code. Everyone in the ground knew that both players, highly popular, were considering their futures. Each miss of that nature brought their sad departures closer.

I looked around me and felt it, the misery, the ennui and the despairing emanations: You would think Notts were three down. Another dreadful afternoon of learned helplessness, the early stages of the Death of Football...

Later, the three of us sat in the pub, and one-by-one the others turned up. Nick, Basford Paul, Little Dave and Haxford. Clifton Tom and his lad. All of them.

We sat drinking with them for a couple of hours, and we talked anything but Notts. One thing I noticed: Not one of them said anything about the absence of HobNob in the past year.

It was as if he had never been away, as if he had not missed a match, as if he had been on every away trip, every Saturday night out, every other social. As if he had been a huge part of it. This was being part of something. It seemed peculiar to me, with my liberal friends, my lecturer pals and writer chums. They would want to discuss the absence. They would acknowledge his disappearance. It was in them. It was in the culture.

There was a level of denial here, almost. And also a layer of disinterest. I noticed that from before. It seemed that a code existed in the group.

What happens outside Notts, stays outside Notts.

And that's where it belongs.

The thought of this comforted me. I imagined a gang of women, and they would want to know every single detail, every day or every week of the absence covered.

Not these guys.

They didn't ask a question about their absences.

It was as if it were a matter of supreme indifference to everyone.

As if they had never been away at all. As if they had actually been there this season at Orient, Crewe, Scunthorpe, United, Pompey and Yeovil. Shrewsbury, Bournemouth, Swindon and Carlisle. As if the *spirit* was all that mattered.

Once a Notts, always a Notts...
Men.
These codes.
This togetherness.

They certainly didn't treat me like that, the lads.

To be perfectly honest, a couple of them were downright...

Brentford Away Part II

The brothers looked at each other as they sat next to the wall outside the stadium.

The state of them. Black, blue and bloody.

Alright, Bull?

Not bad, brother. You?

Yeh, not bad.

You look like bollocks, Bull said.

I'm going to hurt next week, mate.

Me, too.

Bull was having none of the ejection. C'mon, let's go and watch the match, he said, knowing full well that if they were caught in the ground, it was all over.

Surrounded by houses – Griffin Park, an old school stadium built in a community rather than on a greenfield retail park cesspit surrounded by McDonalds, Frankie and Benny's, B&Q – they rose and walked round through empty streets to the away end, an end that was miraculously unguarded. With no barbed wire at the top to keep out interlopers, and an easily accessible brick pillar to climb up onto. The two sprinted and climbed up onto the plinth above the turnstiles, one after another. Jumped into the away end.

If the coppers saw them, they said nothing, and the Notts fans who saw them sitting at the back said nothing. The Bullys sat down, watched the football and licked their wounds. They looked over to their left and saw Sparks and the gang surrounded by yellow-jacketed coppers, the Brentford fans who kicked the brothers to shit now watching the match, a sterile affair, like most matches so far that season. Below Sparks' gang, the Brentford mob stood. Some of Sparks' lads had been thrown out, and it wasn't that surprising to see a few Brentford had been ejected.

At half time, Haxford and the lads came over.

You look a mess, you two, he said, shaking their hands, but neither of them felt the pain, knowing that they would feel like shit for the next week, bruised, and cut and battered, but by-and-large, the spin drying could have been a lot worse than it was. They both knew that the attack on the Brentford end was suicide. There was no way they could win from minute one, and it was piss poor bad planning due to drink and bravado.

But they didn't care. They came, they saw, and they attacked an end.

That would do.

Later, in the back of the transit van, the mood was one of congratulations and victory, and the smells were of testosterone, excitement, trainers, fags, bad pies and stale booze.

Everyone present and correct, the police in West London apparently adopting a soft policy of ejection rather than arrest. The new political regime of paperwork and administration was vexing to the average copper who was usually more content swinging a truncheon into the teeth of a starving miner than tapping on the keys of a back office typewriter.

The High Street was busy with shoppers and shirters coming away from Griffin Park. There had been no sign of the Brentford mob, which were bound to be around somewhere.

Leaving an away pen could often be problematic.

In the seventies, matches were all mixed up, the crowd unsegregated – stand where you want like rugby union.

That didn't last long. Fences went up, and special pens for away supporters were created.

What were away pens for? To protect the home supporters? To safeguard the *away* supporters? What was certain was that segregation made it easier for the local hunters to find their prey with little or no effort. In the seventies, local thugs spotted an opposition supporter because they wore scarves like brightly coloured plumage. After a few well publicised beatings, cuttings, and stabbings (the famous Bradford City fan photo after a visit to Liverpool – two hundred and thirty stitches, a train track down his back from the nape of his neck to the base of his spine, front page news on all the Sundays), you learned when travelling away to ditch the scarf and mingle in.

Shut your cakehole. Don't order a pie from the hatches, don't go to the boozer and don't tell anyone the time if they asked.

Then, the away pen appeared. An away supporter may as well have tattooed himself on the forehead.

**I Am An Opposition Supporter.
Please Kick The Fuck Out Of Me.**

Local thugs could wait outside the away pen on deckchairs and enjoy a pint of beer underneath a pink parasol. Not only did you get the hooligans who had actually *seen* the match, but you got the zombies who spent the day in the pub. The small town morons who couldn't give a flying fuck about their team, who consumed football through Match of the Day and paid only for games involving Man Utd, and Liverpool, and Chelsea, and Tottenham. The plastics. The local headcases who turned out for the fighting. The native thugs. The pubmen, the barflies, the Frank Booths, the furious-hearted alcoholics with their white socks, skinheads, Pods, Pepe jeans, burgundy box jackets, buttery teeth, dripping armpits, low-grade booze, toxic fags, condemned meat pies and solemn, despairing, battered wives.

Four thirty on the dot.

No effort required.

Open the gullet, down the foamy slops in one, and find the away pen.

Take Swindon versus Notts County in August 1985.

Classic example of away pen entrapment in action.

The Robins, recently promoted from the fourth tier, were on a high under Lou Macari. Picture the scene: The ramshackle ground, crowded wooden stands painted Robin Redbreast Red, the Swindon colours, four giant pylons standing sentinel, banks of rocky terraces like urban cliffs, the sun blazing on a high summer day, the first match of the season.

The West Countrymen expected a rout.

The fourth division championship won by March the previous year, and they had every reason to believe that lightning was going to strike twice. The football equivalent of Hitler's iron legions invading the Sudetenland, Czechoslovakia, Poland, Belgium, Holland, France, Greece...not stopping, on a roll, on a buzz. Unbeatable Swindon Stukas in the clouds dive-bombing division three.

The supine enemy: Three hundred subdued Notts huddled in the top corner of the Kop under a silver grey pylon.

Swindon began baying for blood in the opening minutes of the encounter, and they didn't stop for ninety minutes. Shadeys, every one of them. Almost all of them out for the afternoon for the purpose of drinking as much cider as possible and then kicking the fuck out of anything with a northern accent and a black and white heart. Old school Notts fans remembered Leeds in 1975. Stoke at home in 1974. Docherty's Man Utd at home in 1976.

This was similar.

I went to a massacre, and a football match broke out.

Sensible Notts County supporters prayed for their own side to lose and thus, with positive thinking and divine intervention in the vast car park outside the Swindon main stand, the damage inflicted might be limited to a few trips, a swear word or two, a northern cunt, a fucking wanker; the odd rabbit punch.

Three hundred mile round trip and when you get there, you want your team to lose. It seemed strange, but it happened, even if no one admitted to it at the time. The zombie-eyed Swindoners baying for blood. Two thousand of them.

They saw to that.

Naturally, God being a deity with an ironic sense of humour, Notts won 5-1 in what turned out to be the best performance of that entire season.

A result that the baying, drooling ultra-violent Swindon locals were not expecting in the slightest, and it drove them mental.

Most of the thousand-strong hooligans left the ground after three goals and waited menacingly outside, kicking at the doors in a recreation of the zombie apocalypse.

You could see them turn.

You could see their eyes redden.

You could see the bloodlust in their pale faces.

The younger, smaller ones peered through the gaps in-between the two giant red doors to the away pen.

Spitting, shouting.

Rage zombies.

Zuvembi.

The walking shambling dead.

The Notts hooligans – and there weren't many on show that day, Dale Crenshaw, Wilconnen, Alan C, Shaun Church, Sparks, some of the older ARA lads, some Clifton, big Pridge, Clifton Tom, Breaker, Haxford, Clarkson, the Printer, Whisky Jack – knew that there was no chance of survival out there on those streets.

They had been there before.

When a fourth goal went in, rather than cheer, the visitors trapped in the away pen turned around to see the reaction of the mob banging on the doors outside.

The Swindon fans started to sing.

More accurately, they started to chant. A mantra, a hymn, a paean, the hooligan psalm, a homage to the Gods of War, Mars, Aries, the intonation, the universal lad's recitation, both a curse, a wish fulfilment and a prediction.

The Notts hooligans knew it well.

They could hear, loud and clear, the **you're going to get your fucking heads kicked in** song being sung outside.

A simple, repetitive ditty, ideal for masculine get-togethers such as this, with no complicated verses to remember and no need to trail off embarrassingly when you cannot remember the next line. It goes something like this.

You're going to get your fucking heads kicked in!
Clap. Clap. Clap. Clap. Clap Clapaclapaclap.
You're going to get your fucking heads kicked in!
Clap. Clap. Clap. Clap. Clap Clapaclapaclap.
You're going to get your fucking heads kicked in!

Clap. Clap. Clap. Clap. Clap Clapaclapaclap.

Sung by a thousand young men in sportswear. Every one of them believing every single syllable they sang with a passion.

The Notts fans – shirters, scarfers, electrician Tony and his merry band of guzzlers who had just visited an open day at the local brewery. Haxford and his carload, the chap with the fifties slickback, the Weatherman, the fanatic Notts women with oversized purple overcoats carrying picnic baskets, the faceless baldies, the nameless skins, the programme collectors, the subbuteo enthusiasts, the groundhoppers with their wives and girlfriends, the men with the titanic spectacles and their replica green and lemon pinstriped shirts, the miners who hadn't missed a match since Atlee, the old brewery workers, the drunken dribblers and the small knot of hooligans present, about fifteen of them – all felt the liquids inside them turn to ice water.

Thousands of them outside all trying to get in.

Swindon Walking Dead.

They began to push the doors.

You could see the big wooden portals bend, the chains on the handles straining as they tried to force their way in. The coppers on the inside, the thin yellow line, watching and listening like the rest of them...

...but the doors held.

When it was all over, it took the coppers twenty minutes to disperse the locals and rather than open those doors, Notts were marched around the perimeter of an empty ground to the home stands and released through a back entrance. Allowed to scatter among the civilians still wandering around shell-shocked at the results. The Swindon hooligans, a bit slow on the uptake, only worked out what was happening when it was too late.

Most of the Notts fans got away, but it wasn't all Steve McQueen on his motorbike.

A Notts mini-bus was overturned and set on fire. The supporters' coach returned the hundred and thirty miles back up the M5 and M42 with broken windows and no windscreen. Several Notts who lacked the survival skills necessary to survive a situation like this (mingling, whistling, hiding in plain sight), were asked the time on the way back to the train station.

The polite ones received a slap for their good manners. Another was kicked half to death next to an Asian beer-off. Two young theology students in glasses, who didn't even support Notts and were studying at Uni in Bristol, were set upon by frustrated locals and hospitalised.

HobNob mingled in with the local civilians walking in an anaconda-like procession back to the train station. He noticed several other Notts doing the same. He even winked at one and very nearly gave himself away to an ugly looking cider drinker in a red Harrington with ears the size of the tips of broccoli spears, tombstone teeth, and piggy eyes far too close together for decent conversation. Survival was the important thing.

Today, Brentford hadn't turned out like that and getting back to the transport proved easy, like before the match proved easy, none of the Brentford anywhere to be seen. The van pulled away from the kerb and merged into the busy traffic. Progress was slow. One of the ARA lads had bought twenty four cans of Stella, and he passed them round. Surprised, Bull asked Sparks to stop off at the next off licence, and he'd buy the same. A recently qualified electrician, he wasn't short of money, and he was one of those men who paid his way to the penny, and he had an inexhaustible thirst. Sparks, aware of his reputation as a drink-fuelled headbanger nodded and said, okay, Bull, will do, and he then proceeded to pass three off licences in a row while Bull and the gang nattered in the back.

As they reached the top of the High Street, a traffic island, Sparks slammed his foot on the brakes.

Lads! That lot.

Everyone stood and looked through the front window. Fifteen Brentford up ahead and they hadn't seen the van. Blondie and his gang. Cats who had just lapped at the cream. Sportswear and smart cockney haircuts, a spark of colour and clean jeans and white-striped trainers.

Equal numbers, someone said.

(They think they won.)

(Cunts. Cunts.).

(Let's kill em…)

Sparks raised his hand to signal quiet.

Shut it. Let them get past us. We're in a traffic jam…I'll pull over to the side and park…

He did so, pulling the van over outside a Bangladeshi takeaway, which even experienced from inside a malodourous transit, seemed to fill the Hounslow air with cumin, cinnamon, and curry powder.

The Brentford lads hadn't seen the van, and they pulled level on the other side of the road.

Sparks turned away, and his two pals in the front bobbed down.

Chortling and joshing, the Brentford lads walked past.

Ready, boys? Church said, pulling out a decorator's knife.

Everyone averred…

Silence.

Tick. Tick. Tick.

The celestial clock. The warriors clock.

Tick. Tick. Tick.

Ready…

Steady…

THEN, LET'S KILL THE CUNTS…

…back doors flew open, and Notts poured out screaming.

Ahh Across the street, they ran, vaulting over the bonnets of parked cars, snaking in the gaps between Renaults and cabs, Vivas and Fiestas, swooping through gaps between startled pedestrians and powerless wheelchairs.

Instinctively, the Brentford lads started to run, but some stood, and the brave clashed in the front garden of a house upon a lawn you could play snooker on, next to a silver birch tree in full leaf, an Asian family inside observing a joyous Sparks floor Blondie himself, the lad who came up to Meadow Lane, their leader, bang. Pablo Barks kicked another in the head. Older Sparks a double punch, left right, left right. Bull butted another one, another, another, another. Church whacked another, a flash of colour, a vehement kaleidoscope of yellows and cherries, and pinks and lemons, and whites and greens, and cobalt blues. Church cracked one, and then he was nutted to the floor, stunned. Brentford running all over Hounslow, Notts chasing them as far as they could before a Black Maria full of coppers appeared, exultation turned to fear, and the ARA van was quickly surrounded. Everyone with a northern accent quickly snapped up.

Thrown into the back of the paddy wagon.

Saturday afternoon, all over.

HobNob and Bull tried to escape, but were targeted by two young coppers.

These two were in our end. And they got back in the ground, northern plonkers, one said, slapping HobNob round the ears.

Time for a weekend's stay at the station hotel, said the other, chortling, sport for them.

The brothers were thrown in the front of the paddy wagon next to a burly looking old school copper with sideburns.

HobNob sobered up and assessed the situation.

Most of the boys had been arrested on the streets and were in the van. His brother glared at the young copper with the attitude. Church had forgotten to throw away his blade and was shitting it. Sparks laughed with one of the coppers. Their transit van was parked on the side of the road surrounded by coppers. Bystanders over the road watched them and metaphorically gave the police a round of applause.

Hooligans! Good riddance! I hope they throw away the key.

Most of the Brentford had long gone, but HobNob noticed Blondie and his mate giving them the wanker sign from the doorway of a gravyless chip shop.

(Who's the Daddy, northern cunts!)

Getting nicked was not a good move for HobNob and he went into overdrive. He turned to the copper next to him. A sergeant.

Listen, mate. It all got a bit out of hand, but I've got a solution.

Shut it, the sergeant said.

Just up the road, not three minutes away, is the exit to the M25.

Shut it, I said, repeated the sergeant.

There are twenty of us. You can put us in our van, nice and quiet, we'll say sorry for being naughty, you can give us a quick escort past the roundabout, and we'll be out of Hounslow in five minutes flat, and we won't be coming back. No one's been hurt. There's no need for all that nasty paperwork and that. We'll get petrol at Toddington, and we'll be out of your hair and out of your lives. It will be as if we've never been here.

This time, the sergeant didn't repeat himself. Sitting back in his seat, he stared out of the window. He gestured to another copper and got out of the wagon.

Sparks, watching what was going on, gestured to everyone to stay quiet.

The two coppers spoke for five minutes or so, and all was silent in the van. The sergeant popped his head in the window.

Who's the driver? He asked. Sparks nodded.

Been drinking?

No, officer, Sparks said. Teetotal, me.

Get back in your van. We'll take you up to the junction. If I see you again today, you're all nicked. Now, piss off out of my town.

The boys needed no second asking and emptied the wagon faster than they filled it, and they were soon being escorted out of London....

5. Bring me the head of Guatemala Joe

I didn't see the brothers for a week or so, and then, out of the blue, Bull contacted me on my mobile. I had been busy, and their absence wasn't a problem. I had three writing jobs to do – a ghost job for a paranormal erotica story, a blog post on the restored Workhouse in Southwell and an article for a deal-making website on the topic of antique spoons.

The latter was a blag. I knew nothing about spoons, antique or otherwise, when I started writing it and even now, I know nothing about spoons.

(Come to think of it, I know nothing at all about paranormal erotica or the Southwell Workhouse.)

The deal-making website had also contacted me to see if I was interested in two thousand words on the history of tablecloths, but I turned that down – there was no way I could summon the enthusiasm.

Tablecloths?

I was more interested in the antics of the Bully brothers. Tablecloth culture came a poor second in that race. Therefore, I passed it on to an internet-writing pal of mine who took the job with enthusiasm, the starving twenty quid-a-day blog scavenger that he is.

Periodically, I surfed the Internet to see if I could find information about Cedar Forest. I couldn't. Not a word. I heartily wished I had gone inside with Bull just to have a look at the place. I laid in bed on Monday night thinking about it, and I couldn't sleep. It became necessary to take a Temazepam to put me to sleep.

What IS Cedar Forest and why had HobNob been in there?

Yo, Bull started.

How are you?

I'm alright. Just to let you know that there's a demo planned on the last day of the season. Next week.

Trew out?

Nah, that will come later. Have you seen what happened to the Bentinck?

No, I replied.

The Bentinck was a famous old pub next to Midland Station and something of a Nottingham football institution. Almost every Notts fan I spoke to has some story or other connected to the Bentinck and the hostelry is thought of with some affection. As pubs go, for Notts hooligans, this was Stonehenge or if not Stonehenge, then Glastonbury Tor. I wondered whether it had burned down.

They've turned it into a Guatemala Joe's, Bull said.

You're kidding.

Nope. Go down and have a look. Bastards. That's a Notts landmark. We go back years there. The chaps aren't happy. It's full of cunts now – yuppies and students on their iPods and laptops. Sad.

It is.

And annoying. We can't let it go past without some sort of protest.

Anyone protest?

A café owner on Carrington Street complained and objected, but it was overruled. You know how it is with firms like Guatemala's...

...they seem to get carte blanche. Wherever they want. They can have anything.

HobNob says it's yet another example of all-pervasive American Cultural Imperialism. I agree, Mark. It's hard not to agree. Look at the High Street...

It's not good, I replied. I had written an article on the homogenisation of British High Streets not long previously, and I knew the facts. Much of it was due to global franchising pressures, and much of that was coming from America, the home of franchising. Talking to Bull made me think of the article I wrote. I felt passionate about it and thus, the article was well received.

Visiting Nottingham Town Centre wasn't as exciting as it was when we were kids. Victoria Centre was, with the exception of the market, a formulaic miasma of brands. Its sister, Broad Marsh, on the other side of the City, historically a key driver of the retail economy and a place to be seen, had become something of a civic embarrassment with its unoccupied units and chavvy ambience. Every third shop in the City sold mobile phones, punctuated by Gregory's Pasties (at least six branches, based at convenient points around the City, like filling stations on a long and winging road). Chain ladies outfitters. Chain trinket emporia. Chain candle makers. Cafés selling cutely marketed coffee accompanied by home-cooked muffins at scarcely believable prices. American burger joints, American sandwich shops. American waffle houses, cookie franchises and cupcakeries. Guatemala Joe's and the British equivalent, the San Salvador Coffee House. The Italian equivalent, Il Café Caesar. Loads of bookmakers. Supermarket satellites selling high-priced sandwiches. Sportswear houses selling tee shirts for a quid, each one stitched with the tears of little Indonesian girls and the auburn twine of slain Malay Orang-Utans.

Many of the City Centre pubs Nottingham was once famous for had been shut down and replaced by eateries. Pubs like The Exchange, the Bench and Bar, the Horse and Groom, the King John, the legendary Fountain, the compact Dog and Bear, the marbled QEII, the ancient Flying Horse, the Hearty Goodfellow (today, a criminally priced upmarket Indian brasserie), all gone, either boarded up or replaced. PubCo's had taken over – the Ashes and Wallaby, Magic Spoons (whose buying techniques are the stuff of urban myth), the Forest-supporting Sport Billy organisation, with its plastic Sunday afternoon fans and Sky Sports. The Pub and Kitchen brand behind the South Nottingham revival. Myriad gastropubs. Bistros sponsored by top TV chefs charging fifteen quid for a starter.

Independent retailers like Gauntleys, Briddocks and Selectadisc had been wiped out by usurious rentals charged by London-based property conglomerates. Pearsons and Habitat, merchants housed in quality temples of stone and marble, gone. All the comic shops had shut down.

Despite murmurings from the City Council, nothing changes. The trendy, transmetropolitan "Hub" approach to retail, a civic proclamation bordering on dogma. Most of the key players at the Council House went to the same University in the eighties, Trent, then stayed here and built lucrative political careers. Most of them have no childhood connection to Nottingham, nor its retail status as the Queen of the Midlands, no memories of how it used to be. Thus, they have nothing emotionally substantive to invest in the economic diversity of the City Centre.

Blandness reigns.

Exceptions – Bridlesmith Gate is supposed to be the fourth best shopping street in the country for expensive clothes and Hockley is still a figment of cultural consciousness, but the City Centre itself? An anaemic souk of jigsaw chains and needy franchises.

Bull changed the subject back to where we started.

Are you coming to the protest? It's going to be proper naughty. Good for your book.

When is it? I replied.

Last match, in two or three weeks. Last weekend in April.

I'll be there.

If I don't see you before, we can meet at Fellows. Have a few ales, get in the mood. And there'll be some Coventry about – not that we're interested in all that, he said.

Of course not, I replied. How's HobNob? Did he get that job?

They're checking references. And guess what?

What?

He's got a date tomorrow night!

Hah! A date…

Yep. An old bird of his. He's been nattering to her on the interweb, plucked up the courage.

I wonder whether she's anything like Aunty Britney.

I doubt it. Aunty Britney's unique, he laughed.

Hahah…yep.

A job and a bird. All he needs is a gaff, all being well. I know someone who is moving out of his place. I've already had a word. The hat trick.

Mate, this is top news. I'm buzzing for him. It must be tough to start over.

He's done it before, and he'll do it in the future. My brother is that type of bloke. Up and down.

Is he?

Not straight forward.

Up and down.

Like a roller coaster. He's out with his lad tomorrow. Mini-Beefy. Buffet.

Which one?

Red Hot, I think.

The best one. You're making me hungry.

Bonus. I think I'll get myself a Maccy Ds. See you in Fellows next week. It'll be a giggle.

I'll see you there.

Yeh, cheers, he said, putting the phone down.

The Garden of England
Gravesend and Ebbsfleet

HobNob: *Let me tell you about the second time I went to Kent. The first time comes later. I know that might seem odd and something of a digression, but you need Clarkson to clarify some details about that horror second trip before we start. Alright? Anyway, 2003. I travelled down to see Notts play Gravesend and Ebbsfleet in the first round of the FA Cup*

A Saturday afternoon in December 2003

Kent.

They call it the Garden of England.

Was it Chaucer who labelled it thus? Did you know that Chaucer intended *Canterbury Tales* to be something like three hundred tales long, but he died a quarter of the way through? No? I'm not sure where I heard that. Is it true? It ought to be.

When I was a kid, I never visited Kent. From that Garden description, I built up a mental image of the place. Orchards, trees bursting with pears, peaches, apples, plums and figs. Rolling hills and jade farmland. Horses gambolling in summer meadows. Cows grazing contentedly in emerald pastures. The estuary; sea gulls announcing their entrance to the shore with a stridency of relentless squawks. Kittiwakes escaping stormy turbulence in the Channel. I don't think we even went to Dover as a family. Bull doesn't remember us visiting. I certainly can't remember it, and I certainly can't recall Kent, even if we did.

When we went to Gillingham in October, 1987, one of our first train trips with the boys we'd met at Bristol City – Clarkson, The Printer, Breaker, Haxford, Little Dave, that lot, a few others we didn't know very well – I was expecting the Darling Buds of May.

But we'll come to that later.

My life had just begun to rebuild itself after six terrible years. Mini-Beefy, my lad, and I were going to matches together – I took him to Darlo and Wrexham in the car, places like that. He'd got seriously into Notts after Stockport away, of all places – but for one reason or another, he couldn't make the trip to Gravesend. He was seven at the time – I think he probably had a kid's party or something. Bull and I were in one of our periodic incommunicado situations – he might have been in Baku, Tashkent, Delhi, or somewhere exotic, so I travelled down on the train alone, down to St Pancras, across London and eastwards through Kent. Nowadays, you get those brilliant scooter trains from St Pancras that take about forty minutes to reach the East Coast – the estuary, Sheerness – but I can't remember which station catered for Kent at that time.

The train was a trundler; I know that, old and slow, a rattler through the City, past Charlton Athletic's ground, through some of the roughest estates you have ever seen in your life on the outskirts of the capital. Delinquent overspill. All the dwellings jammed together *in all directions* – not just rows of terraces, but buildings *overhanging* each other, a surreal jigsaw, patched up throwaway design. Houses *on top* of houses. Thousands of them. Literally thousands upon thousands of abodes without any apparent space between them in any dimension. I know this isn't possible, but that's how it *seemed*. I remember it being the first time I had seen blocks of flats painted like rainbow mosaics, lovely optimistic colours on the skyline. The local authority goes to all that trouble to regenerate these flats and the locals carry on, hanging their rancid smalls out of the windows! I can't understand that in the age of tumble dryers. I just can't get to the bottom of that at all.

My overall impression was that the passage to Gravesend was one unlimited industrial / residential wasteland. High-rise flats. Exhausted, worn-out, derelict, burnt-out industrial parks. Featureless warehouses. Bad tags, lifeless graffiti. More of those stickle brick pile ups, and flats along the side of the railway that seemed as if they had been *bolted on* to the railway platforms itself.

Do you know what I didn't see?

Anything *green*.

No orchards, no rows of trees, no kids jumping from trees onto harvested hay bales, no undulating acres, no lush hillsides. Where is the Garden? I couldn't see it. The landlords of the shanty houses along the railway had over concreted, probably to convert lawn to driveway, or because they couldn't be bothered to maintain overgrowth in unoccupied properties. That journey, even more than Gillingham earlier, established just how *ungardenlike* Kent is.

It all made me think what a shitty country we live in.

What a completely *ugly* country.

Everyone thinks of Stratford-Upon-Avon, but not the *other* Stratford, a spectacular cement shithole. I realised that I wasn't going to be witnessing Yeoman Hearts of Oak crunching carrots and chewing straw on country stiles.

I remember the weather. Pewter skies, a howling wind – it all made the journey across West Kent seem somehow, apocalyptic. By the time I left the train at Gravesend station, it was getting dark. Foggy. There was a funk in the air, a reek, an aroma of chlorine and sulphur suspended above the churning, grinding wind.

Strangest thing: I don't know why, but I was bricking it.

Maybe it was the view on the way in, all blitz décor, mangled pylons and asphyxiated scrub.

Welcome to Kent. Hope you survive the experience.

I'd not yet bought a drink. I was going out with a woman in London in the evening, a nice woman I'd met on the Internet and I didn't want to turn up bladdered for a first date. Besides, I thought I was on a promise, and I didn't want to let her down when it mattered. I'd planned to enjoy a pint or two at the ground before the event, and that would be it. You know how hard it is to be at Notts sober, and I always used to enjoy a pint before an away trip to prepare for the fighting; this sobriety was a rare state, and the lack of booze was amplifying my anxiety.

For one moment, I nearly turned back to London. Called up my date and offered to meet her early for a bite to eat. After all, who knew I was coming to Gravesend? I'd lost touch with the gang. I wouldn't lose face. Bull would never know and neither, in the future, would Mini-Beefy. Truth was, I genuinely wanted to see that match. Get the ground in. Fuck Man Utd versus Man City on the telly with all the plastics, all the students.

That match was *real* football.

(Anyway, enough football politics: You know how I feel about plastics.)

Gravesend Station is a shithole, and the whole Kent thing was starting to give me the willies. One time, Bull and I went to The Den on the train, and we went boozing on that council estate near the ground – I know, I know, we were young and reckless – and I was feeling just like that as if I was going to get *disembowelled* the moment I left the fucking station!

Gravesend Station was not a nice place, believe me.

However, I pinched myself, pulled up my breeches, inflated my bollocks and walked over into the concourse where amazingly, proving that the human brain has more than five senses, I saw this geezer, some crackhead, skinny, emaciated, in a red baseball cap, smacking the shit out of another crackhead by a ticket machine.

The victim elevated each time a blow connected each whack that landed. A little float. Good punches, proper clouts, sickening cracks echoing round the ticketing area. Two birds – chavvy fuckers, tattoos, stinky mingers, dirty tats, hair in ponytails – were screaming at the aggressor to stop hitting the other bloke whose nose was exploding and who was on the verge of losing consciousness. One of the women, tattooed to the gills and wearing a sickeningly revealing flesh coloured vest despite the frigid temperature, had her *kid* with her, four or five years old, in a pushchair worth a monkey, maybe even two monkeys, a Ferrari pushchair or something like that.

Jesus, it was a scene and a half.

Do you know what I did?

I walked past them all toward the taxi rank as if that unfortunate British Saturday afternoon disagreement *wasn't happening* – as if this was a phantasm, an illusion, a fevered reverie spawned by my oversensitive unconscious.

I almost whistled!

You know, like Norman Wisdom used to do.

Nothing to do with me, mate!

No one noticed me. This was family business in Gravesend. My heart was racing. I didn't want to be laid out by that bony-knuckled crackhead – or that tattooed chav chick, to be honest.

A modern family out on a Saturday afternoon. Shopping for kids clothes. A new bubble lamp for the front room. A bite to eat. Fresh veg and fruit for the kids. A new Tom

Cruise DVD. Knick-knacks from the Pound Goblin. The IKEA sale further down the line in Rochester.

Ten years on, I can *hear* the sound those punches made. Like a whip crack. I don't mind telling you, and I've told you before. I don't mind a football punch-up because there are codes, and rules, and structures, but this kind of naked violence inflicted by underclass surfers like this, junkies who've had the checks-and-balances meter in their brain blown out by coke and speed, no – no chance. They give me the willies. There's a fat hooli who follows Bury who got himself into all sorts of bother a few years back at Notts, at the station. Makes Buster Bloodvessel look like Kate Moss. I don't know what the bother was, but it took four coppers to bring him down. Big ugly coppers, not them kids they recruit today. Proper thugs, riot coppers.

Clockwork Oranges.

I would rather be smacked by *him* than this cracksnaffler at Gravesend. Buster wouldn't kill you deliberately, and the mass of his punch would be spread across the whole area of the impact zone.

This Gravesend crackhead?

All knuckles, angles and sharp points. No way, Jose. No fucking way.

And his expression? Jesus. Hatred. Unadorned, undressed, unadultered hatred. For all I know, that afternoon he could have killed his mate, his brother, his love rival, whoever it was, but by the time of potential death, I was in a black cab telling my man to take me to the ground.

Kent, huh.

The Garden of England.

The Garden of Darkness, more like.

The pub nearest the ground wasn't friendly – full of cockneys, townies, Kentishmen and pissheads, all in a confined space – especially when Haxford's coach pulled up right outside. Most Notts on the coach went straight to the stadium, but Breaker, Basford Paul, Sea Monster, Clifton Tom and Haxford himself, came in for a quick one before kick off. I saw some hooli in a Tottenham shirt pull out his blower and use the word "lads." When he did that, I knew we were in a different zone altogether.

Notts lads picked up the vibe. A couple I didn't know well drank up, left. It wasn't worth coming down here to get lifted before the game. Those days were over by this time, especially as we are all over forty and some of us pushing fifty. By now, in early December, it was grim outside. Gravesend and Ebbsfleet's ground was one big pile of merde in the fulcrum of one of those infinite A-Roads that cross Kent and Essex, which all lead to London. The stadium had been surrounded by a giant billboard as if it was being developed. The only light outside the pub came from passing cars, the ground's floodlights, and the retail estate over the island.

In the pub, their lads played pool.

Tasty-looking fuckers: capped up, trainers.

They were up for it, but somehow, coppers appeared, and that took the edge off the atmosphere, and the Notts lads departed. I followed, nattering to Clifton Tom and Breaker. We kept looking behind us to see whether we had been followed – and I heard later that two or three other lads I didn't know took a punch or two in the car park – but there was nothing doing for us. I much prefer fighting in the sunshine. It shits me up, fighting in the dark on away trips – Wigan away, for example. You have no idea where you are, and you're completely at the mercy of the locals who can navigate the streets around their manor blindfolded.

Walking to the match from that pub was fucking eerie – despite the cars, it seemed silent, like a murky wood – and I was glad to get in the ground, to be honest. I think everyone was. I'd much rather travel north. You know where you stand – here, down south, anything could happen!

We beat the plucky Kentishmen 1-0 in the 94th minute, which wouldn't have gone down well with the locals. Clive Platt's finest moment in a black and white shirt. Naturally, we tried to invade the pitch in our glee – average age, forty – but the coppers were wise to it. Plod had both Haxford's coach and the supporters coach right outside the ground, and as it was full-blown night, I merged in with the baying

Gravesend locals and headed up that interminable A road toward the station.

To save taxi fare (the one to the ground cost me an arm and a leg), I planned to walk all the way to the station, a good three quarters of an hour, but as I walked, I realised that this was probably a bad idea.

A *really* bad idea.

No one asks you the time anymore, but there were gangs of lads hanging about on every corner, and they all seemed to be looking at me. Row after row of High Rise flats skirted the A-Road, and these local meatheads weren't members of the Gravesend and Ebbsfleet official supporters club. Rappers, muggers, robbers, fighters and beaters, hooded young bravos with fuck all to do but batter strangers from the North. Given the chance they would hammer you, shiv you, leave you half dead under a streetlamp and disappear in a puff of smoke as if they had never existed.

One group in particular, sitting on a wall outside a Community Centre hut, which looked abandoned and shut, seemed to pay me plenty of attention. Multi-cultural, nihilistic, enraged, disenfranchised young flat-dwellers, hooded and trackied to fuck. There didn't seem to be a bus stop or anywhere to flag down a taxi, but up ahead, I saw a train station sign. I crossed the road away from the flats and headed towards it. A minor station that would feed the bigger one at which I had arrived.

The Kent evening was piercing; there was a nippy wind building up, and I genuinely didn't want to be there. Added to that, there was the encroaching darkness and mist that got thicker the further you walked away from the stadium, the emanations from the floodlights receding into the distance. Jesus. No shops with comforting lit displays. Not even an Asian newsagent. Streetlights cast what little radiance there was. Dipped beams from passing cars flickered sporadically. Behind me, pedestrian signals curtailed the oncoming traffic heading to the Town Centre; there was no illumination at all.

Space black.

And all the time, this particular mob was watching me.

I could tell. I could feel the stares. I could sense the collective decision making. S*hall we? Shall we not? Shall we? Shall we not?* In my day, I didn't mind fighting casuals and shadeys, but streetfighters and townies – the codes are different.

And I knew these boys would slice me up. Just knew it.

My bollocks shrivelled, and my arse wobbled. My belly went a rubbery one. I seemed to be the only fella wandering the road, definitely the only Notts, and the traffic seemed to die down. This was shitty. In general, being loners, Bull and I are not mad keen on coaches, and big expeditions – I'd hate following a big club like United because there are lads everywhere and your identity is like subsumed into one great big whole, like locusts, like ants – but there were times, and this was one, where being part of a major firm would have major fuck off advantages: that road outside Gravesend and Ebbsfleet was one of those times.

I wasn't enjoying my day out in the Garden of England at all and couldn't wait to get back to London.

This was the Boondocks, the Outback, the Swamps, only with trees of concrete, slabs instead of earth, and natives with Stanleys instead of poison arrows.

The temptation to jog was strong, but I just ambled along as if I owned the place. Chest out. Head up. Hiding in plain sight – running would have been stupid, a sign glowing above my head; **I Am Prey, Please Eat Me** – and eventually, I reached the station and took a turn into the entrance.

The station was down a flight of forty, fifty steps. Half-lit a constellation of shadows. A canopy of overgrown foliage spread over the concrete staircase, supported by unkempt, abandoned hedges, rampant nettles and strange, tangled urban weeds. It was hard to tell whether the train station was live, and I hesitated on the top step.

Then, I looked behind me at the posse of lads.

You ever read *The Shining*? You must have.

Everyone's read *The Shining*.

Anyway, Danny, the protagonist, a kid with psychic powers, is out in the hotel playground in the snow. The playground is skirted by sculpted hedge animals – a lion, a tiger – and every time Danny looked round, they seemed to be getting a little bit closer. Just a little bit. He would look away and then back, and each time they would be closer.

Closer.

Well, I felt like that about them lads outside the flats.

Two choices.

Walk down this suicidal staircase in the dark to a train station, which may not exist, may not be active, or get back on the road and get stabbed.

I started to walk down the staircase to the train station at the bottom.

Sometimes, I would have to duck under a branch or step over a bunch of nettles. I tripped over some scrub and nearly fell, but I held on to the guard rail for dear life and eventually, I reached the bottom and walked onto the platform.

The station was little more than a brick hut with a poster timetable, and a long covered open-air waiting area lined with benches. This extended towards a doorway and stopped before restarting on the other side. This was one of those little stations, which survived Beeching in the fifties, and it looked like it had not been maintained since. No one waited on the other side for a train east. I could see people on the other side of the platform, farthest away from the bottom of the staircase and I started to walk toward them for some unknown reason and then…then…after I'd walked five or six paces, I stopped. I don't know why I stopped – some sixth sense and boy, was I paranoid that evening – and stepped back into the waiting area.

I'd not been seen.

At least, I didn't think so.

Carefully, I peeked out from my shelter and had a look at those people at the far end of the platform. It seemed like eight or nine men, homeless, tramps, streetlivers, travellers. They definitely weren't passengers waiting for a train, and I knew that this was a disused station and trains travelled straight past. I'd made an error.

The men were having a drinks party, a White Lightning and Meths party. Two of them held each other in the middle of the platform. They were plastered and holding each other up for support. Or they were dancing, a bizarre Tango with no music.

Someone applauded, a younger lad.

Another tramp with dreads started to shout something I didn't recognise. Another two fellas got up and started to dance, and these two this time, started to snog each other as they danced. Then…then…jeez, one of them started to take his filthy jeans down…you think I'm making this up? This is kosher – I had stumbled onto a Homosexual Wino Party in the Garden of England, and my insides turned to shit and ice.

Before any contact was made between unwashed bodies and without further ado, I braced myself and ran back toward the staircase. Forget the lads on the road – I'd rather have a Frankenstein mush than have these filthy cunts pounding Satan's Dark Cavern like something out of *Deliverance: The Sequel,* and with their shouts and curses in my ear, I sprinted up the stairs like a much younger – and thinner – man, and without turning to look at the road to see whether the hooded bandits were anywhere about, I sprinted as fast as my little legs would carry me until I saw a bus stop with normal people forming an orderly queue.

I joined it.

Paid three quid to get on the next bus to get to Gravesend station and believe me, that was the most joyous three quid I had ever spent.

No kidding.

Fuck me. That was intense.

Completely intense and a little bit sick.

Anyway, just to top off, even more peculiar than all this, I sat with Darren Caskey on the train back to London, and the two of us had a jolly old natter.

He'd just played and had a good game controlling things in the middle of the park. I quite liked him, and we chatted about various matters. I didn't tell him about my walk home in the darkness or the sights I had seen on the platform of that ghost station. I didn't think he would be interested. Instead, we talked about the match, London, women and matters Notts. I learned nothing about Notts I didn't already know, to be honest. He seemed like good company, and I enjoyed the forty-five minute journey.

Pity he turned out to be a complete cunt.

6. Red Hot World

HobNob's best friend was a sixteen year old boy, his son, Mini-Beefy.

He had been given his nickname as a seven year old by an old girlfriend of his dad who remarked on his power-packed size. Stocky, short and bulky then; he had grown tall and lean as time passed by, until today as the two of them gave each other high-fives outside the Ladbrokes on the south side of Victoria Centre, he was actually taller than his father.

Not that that would be difficult.

Dressed in jeans, a Helly Hansen black sports blouson, trainers of a brand his dad didn't recognise, he had lost weight since the last time, a good half a stone. Blonde and handsome, it was often remarked that it was fortunate that he had inherited his mother's looks and his dad's brains rather than the other way round.

Beefster, his dad said. How are you, son?

I'm fine, dad. How are you?

Not bad, son. Been training?

Three times a week, Mini-Beefy replied casually.

Because of his father's stay at Cedar Forest, the two had not seen each other for months, but the reunion wasn't emotional, in the sense of outwardly cloying.

Two years ago, it might have been, but now, Mini-Beefy had become his own man. At one time, father and son met every weekend and had done for a decade, even longer. At Easter, in Whit week, and in the six weeks summer holidays, he would come over to his dad's for a week, and rather than being forced by his mother at gunpoint, like some lads in his situation, he actually wanted to do it. Things changed. At fourteen, friends and a new girlfriend came first. It took a while for HobNob to adjust, but adjust he did.

How's your mother? HobNob asked.

Not bad, not bad.

She got a new chap?

Yeh. Nice bloke. Big on music. Biker. Richie...

Do you get on with him?

He's alright, yeh.

I've never understood that about your mother. Bloody hates heavy metal and always finds herself going out with metalheads.

Haha. That's true.

After the small talk was over, as they walked down Bridlesmith Gate, the busiest shopping street in Europe teeming with eager shoppers, they got down to business.

What did you think of Curle?

He was a tosser, dad. You haven't missed anything.

So your uncle said.

Gates have collapsed. The matches are boring. It's his fault…

Who? Curle or Chairman Trew…

Curle…

What do you think of CK?

Jury's out, dad. Looks much the same to me. Fans aren't happy.

His son was a proper Notts fan in a world where all his friends played X-Box or supported plastic teams that only exist on TV – Man Utd, Arsenal, Chelsea. Or because he lived in Amber Valley, Derby County.

By twelve, he had chalked up fifty grounds, including becalmed Field Mill, Sincil Bank, Blundell Park, Edgeley Park, the George Walker Stadium, Wrexham, Rushden (twice). He had witnessed Notts at Chelsea, Wigan (twice), Fulham, Sunderland and Man City (that was boring). He had already been warned by stewards for sitting on the billboards at Grimsby (a chip off the old block).

Like many hardcore Notts, he hardly ever watched England, had never seen an EPL match all the way through, and he detested Forest.

The two of them chatted away as they walked to the Red Hot World buffet for dinner. On Thurland Street, they ambled past the Thurland Hall, a spectacular dive, an old-fashioned drinker going back to Victorian times. A fine old pub fallen, like so many, on hard times. Inside its sonorous maw were one long circular bar and a froth stained wooden floor. Sitting outside, traditional Nottingham drinkers; mostly old Forest, Mad Squad, Randall's Vandals, St Ann's, Sneinton, A-Block. Skinheaded, ear-ringed, pockmarked, prison-tattooed, strident, vociferous, blind drunk. In some cases, one baby step away from living on the street. A Forest pub through and through: Notts fans tended to avoid it. A few years ago, Forest had been promoted from League One and the celebrations outside the Thurland went on long into the night. Every ex-Forest madboy turned up that night. HobNob and Bull who had been up at Chesterfield, walked past and winked at a few of them, but mostly, it was pointless fighting with Forest, Notts being a supplanted ethnic minority and patronised unmercifully because of it.

Turning the corner toward Hockley, HobNob stopped to put a bet on at the Ladbrokes – a tenner on some unlikely third favourite up at Market Rasen – while Mini-Beefy waited outside.

Full of nostalgia, inspired by both his son and the environment, and like an old man sitting on a park bench, he began to wax lyrical.

We used to drink a lot round here, Beefy. All the gang, every Saturday night. Well, it was more like Thursday night to Sunday night with Saturday and Sunday dinner thrown in. We were always in the pub. Different world: You're not much of a drinker, are you, he said, more of a statement than a question.

Not really, dad. Go out now and again. Round our way.

I was at it from sixteen in the Polish Club in Carrington. The Druids in Arnold. The White Hart. They didn't seem to mind. Keep your mouth shut, keep your wallet open and landlords turned a blind eye. If you didn't upset people on the way home, the coppers left you alone.

Did they ask you for ID?

No, son. No ID. Never carried any. They took your word for it. If you said you were eighteen, they served you. That was an age of trust, words as bonds.

But you were lying, dad!

Only white lies, son, HobNob grinned. There were loads of pubs round here we used to go to. Here, look. The

Bodega. Two floors of Saturday night debauchery. Loads of women in there. If you wanted to go out and pull, the Bodega was the place to go. Tons of bouncers. It's like Hooke's Law or something out of Newton: Wherever there are large numbers of women, there are large numbers of bouncers. Used to go there every time we went out. Great sound system and clean beer. Then, there was the Malthouse, now the Pit and the Pendulum, which featured in *Ultra Violence*, where the unnamed narrator met Beanie, the hyper-cynical hooligan who sets everyone on the road to hell.

I like those bits, Mini-Beefy said. Preferred the fighting chapters, to be honest.

I don't think the book would have been the same without the framing story, Beef.

I know, dad, he replied.

HobNob knew that apart from the ones who hated the book, there were two camps developing. Those who liked the framing story – with the job, Margot, Rita and Perry, and the unnamed narrator's descent into Hell – and those who read it for the fighting chapters. Mini-Beefy was, apparently, in the latter camp.

Mini-Beefy nodded, munched on a bag of Haribos.

Father and son walked up into Hockley, past the Amigos kebab house, past Levins, the high-end diamond dealers and the Cantonese eaterie where the Cantonese themselves eat. Past Spandex Sammy's, the trendy gym, always packed, and the all-you-can-eat Starving Stallion. People ambled by, an endless flow, some towards Hockley, some emerging from there – with yashmaks and burkas, shopping bags and buggys, pushchairs and mountain bikes, skateboards and iPhones. Smoothly and silently, the tram glided in an arc across the long shadows of buildings with newly stone-blasted Edwardian facades. The magnificent Gentleman's Casino, all the upmarket brands, all the Lacostes and White Stuffs, all the Diesels and Benettons. Spotlessly clean, modern, chrome and steel, laminated and polished, incongruously embedded in disused banks. Dickensian brokerages made of incredible stone.

They crossed the road toward an old bookies, now a supermarket satellite and stopped in front of a boarded-up pub, a chalk-face portico.

There's the Lord Nelson, HobNob pointed out.

...the one with the crap music...

It's true. Never heard a decent record in there, all that eighties crap. What a terrible decade for music that was! Music that came out of a tin and sounded like it. New Romantic bollocks and Thatcherite aspirational pop. Drek. Horrible beer – I drank bottled Pils in there, that, or Red Stripe – because their lager tasted like goat's piss. The landlord was a total nob who couldn't keep his beer properly.

He pointed to a hotel with sign intact, about thirty yards down, on the left.

There's the George Hotel. Skully and I used to go in there with all his mates.

Forest lads?

That's right. I didn't often speak, but Skull knew most of them, being Forest.

Mum sees Skull about.

I know, but I've not seen him for donkeys. He's my second oldest friend. I should contact him, but it's difficult to keep friendships going at our age, Beef.

I bet it is, dad.

I remember one night in there, three Notts lads who had just come back from Dusseldorf, were telling me they had been involved in a game of tear-gas tennis with the German coppers at the European Championships. Eighty eight. It was a full service hotel, that. Room service and bell boys. Like many hotels of this type, the George has been murdered by the Dick Whittington Inn and Wonderful Nights. Cheap and cheerful. Just down a bit, look, there's Browne's wine bar, where you went if you wanted to impress a bird. You couldn't pull in there – well, I couldn't pull anywhere! – as it was full of couples drinking Barolo and listening to Curtis Steigers.

Who, dad?

Some curly haired balladeer. Girl's music, soft and soulful. Michael Bolton-ish.

You've got me here, dad, Mini-Beefy said. I've no idea who you are talking about. Are they any good?

Shit, but if you had a woman on the go, listening to ballads like one sung by Steigers, normally put them in a good mood. Worth having your ears pummelled for an hour or two. Trendiest place in Notts for a while. Shut down now…we'll pass it on the way. You hungry?

Starving.

Yep. What are you having? Predominantly Indian or predominantly Chinese?

Predominantly Chinese, dad, I think.

Good choice.

Hockley is the shopping street of choice for all Nottingham's students and young transmetropolitans, with its eye-wateringly expensive designers, its extraordinary boutiques, its eccentric milliners, stubborn cobblers, high-end confectioners, gothic raptures, EMO bazaars, eclectic jamborees and plethora of coiffeurs – some charging up to thirty seven pounds for a gent's short back and sides.

Thirty seven pounds.

They discussed this, stopping outside Jerome's, a charcoal and silvered imbroglio, with an astonishingly sparkling windowpane the full height of the frontage. It appeared to be more like a nightclub than a barber, all seats occupied, six men waiting, reading papers and playing Crash Bandicoot on complimentary Playstations.

This barber here, Beefster. Look at the price.

I know. I can see. Thirty seven quid.

Thirty seven quid for a haircut.

And there's a queue, dad. You tell me this every time.

Do I?

Yes, you do, dad. Thirty seven quid for a just out of bed haircut. Your mate wrote about it in *Ultra Violence*.

Yes, he did.

Mini-Beefy grinned. Next thing you'll be telling me about is the criminally priced return ticket on the Skylink to the airport.

Eight quid. It's incredible. Eight quid.

Oh, and the just out of bed haircut is now out of fashion. The new trendy haircut is the one Danny Craig has in the new Bond.

Skyfall?

That's the one. Still thirty seven quid, dad, but a different cut, Mini-Beefy said, wryly grinning.

I could *never* pay thirty seven quid for a haircut, HobNob replied.

Two young men in matching black short-sleeved shirts, winklepicker shoes and impossibly tight black trousers walked past and into the shop. They heard HobNob. One of them winked at him.

Cheeky...

...come on, dad, I'm starving.

They walked past Stoney Street, and The Angel – where HobNob spent Christmas Day a few years ago in one of his trenches of despair – and the Left Lion offices, underneath a training centre for pole dancers.

Stoney Street is Hockley's border, an invisible line, like the border between Iraq and Iran, evanescent, permeable, indistinct, a cut-off point where Hockley ceases to be bijou and desirable, a place to be seen, a place to swank, and becomes Nottingham again – threadbare, tacky and worn out. The transformation happens quickly: England's bipolarity writ large.

One minute you are walking past a pair of beautiful Scandinavian-looking women with moussed blonde hair, golden jewellery that would shame Croesus, fur coats of dazzling, febrile colour, talking into iPods and tottering about on three hundred quid a pair stripper heels, and the next, in the blink of an eye, without knowing how, as if you had gone through an unsettling jump in the space-time continuum, you are in the middle of a punch-up between two homeless arguing over a hat while standing outside an off licence that has no business being there.

An anomaly, a border oddity.

There is a porn joint that sells vibrators with names (including one called Modok because of its oversized head), and a kebab palace that never closes, not even for Christmas Day. At the bottom, is the dirtiest charity shop in the City, servicing the biggest homeless hostel outside London. At the outer limits of Hockley, there is the decadent (and very dead) Berlins Bar, which in turn, signals the beginning of the politically mythical Southside Corridor.

That's a sight. Boarded up for over a decade and a half after an eighties decade of serving the cheapest drinks possible (and hosting some of Nottingham's most evil fights), Berlins is an eyesore, yet, as HobNob told Mini-Beefy, they would have sorted it had the money to develop the area not been sequestrated by the wicked Tories and the middle class southern establishment.

Never mind, he said, in conclusion, there is always the Red Hot World Buffet House, and for that, we will always be grateful...

Sociogeography lesson over, the two entered the buffet and were escorted by a stunning blonde waitress to a seat by the window. They started talking Notts – about Ian "Charlie" McParland, the Magpies legend from the Warnock era who's stewardship of Notts is the subject of fierce debate amongst locals.

Some venerate his uncompromising dedication to fine football played to feet the Dutch way, his total football approach.

Other more practical supporters remember the Scotsman almost taking Notts out of the football league.

As they ate quietly, concentrating, HobNob thought about his son's history with Notts.

His first trip to Meadow Lane was Notts V Darlington in late ninety seven. Six months old and in a purple car seat. Notts' steady post-Warnock decline had continued, and there was plenty of room in the Pavis for him and his father to sit. Even though the match took place in front of a shirt-sleeved audience in warm sunshine, it was another monotonous affair, Mini-Beefy didn't notice. It could have been the most exciting match ever as far as he was concerned.

Snuggly in his romper suit, decorated with green wizards and indigo parrots, he spent the first half drifting in and out of sleep and the first ten minutes of the second half screaming; at which point HobNob decided that enough was enough.

Over the next six years, HobNob took him to the Lane when he could. Uncle Bull's career continued to blossom, but he made occasional trips to the Cathedral. As did Mini-Beefy's granddad. The club's decline continued under Gary Brazil, the excoriated Gary Mills and the dour old stager Billy Dearden. The painfully slow descent seemed inevitable, and the reasons, from the moment Old Baggy Green Sweatshirt took over the City Ground hotseat in the mid-seventies, were always the same: The existence of Nottingham Forest, not a stone's throw away from the Lane, attracting the lion's share of the City's football supporters. Relatively high admission prices. Competition from one of the country's most robust amateur football leagues. An unattractive product fighting a losing with the Nottingham public's transforming expectations. There was never enough money. Not enough Notts fans coming to watch, the benchmark 8,000 a distant memory, sometimes even for decent games.

Mini-Beefy took a while to be convinced of the glory of Notts County.

For the first six years of his life, he responded to the prospect of visiting Meadow Lane with a surly, almost mardy distaste. He even came to HobNob's flat one day with ideas of following Man United like all his friends at school before a heartbroken HobNob got to work with his mobile phone. After revealing the news of his changed allegiance, Beef sat eating his fruit pieces and yoghurt, watching Johnny Bravo on the cartoon channel. HobNob picked up his phone, and making sure his son could see and hear, pretended to call a friend in Manchester who was looking for a son.

Would he like one?

He would sell Beef for a hundred pounds cash. While he would be sad to see Beef go, a father who followed Manchester United was what he wanted. After all, HobNob said into the silent phone ostentatiously, a son should always follow the same team as his father, and grandfather, and also *his* father and grandfather.

Beef, hearing this and looking shocked, promptly burst into tears.

After saying sorry and receiving assurances from his father that he wasn't actually going to sell him to a new dad, he never repeated his talk about Man United

Dutifully, ever since that day, he would go to Meadow Lane with his dad, like countless young boys before him, aware of some of the most important cultural information in the country.

Great Grandad.

Grandad.

Dad.

Sons.

Grandsons.

Cultural History you didn't need a history A'level to understand.

One day, it clicked for him.

Like clockwork, a lever pressed, the final jigsaw piece, Mini-Beefy became a Notts fan. He was seven years old. Stockport. At poor, doomed, Stockport. His blue puffa jacket. A couple of hundred Notts in the seats. Two one down, second half, a winter's day, his dad and uncle present. Like most of the followers, he was riveted by an unusually end-to-end game of football. HobNob tried to entertain him with jokes and a running commentary, but there was no need – Mini-Beefy was hypnotised by the match. For the first time. Cheering, shouting, clapping (which he never usually did), exhorting. It seemed to happen by magic and HobNob had never felt such pride – not even when his son was born. Notts equalised and Mini-Beefy went mad, running up and down the gangway, fists raised in triumph as if Santa had delivered all the toys on his Christmas list a month early.

A Notts fan forever.

Some kids never experience that – the instant gratification of TV nullifying all the pain Mini-Beefy went through in the early years; the tedium, the cold, the pointlessness of ninety minutes of football taking place in front of five thousand despairing supporters. To feel the joy with football, you have to experience an awful lot of pain – financial (the admission prices), physical (the elements), emotional (losing in extra time at West Ham away on a Tuesday night in the cup, a Lee Chapman fluke, the long journey home), and philosophical (I could have done something *exciting* rather than watching this) – and Mini-Beefy experienced that, getting the payoff at Edgeley Park that day.

As HobNob munched on a slice of Naan, he thought about the upcoming meeting at the Bentinck. He had pondered long and hard about whether to invite Mini-Beefy or not.

Last matches of the season, even in recent times, are sometimes brutal. Wycombe, last year, saw the biggest turnout of Notts lads for several years. Chesterfield away punctuated by skirmishes around The Industry and the train station. Beef was there for that one, and the Bury match in 2006 where a bad result at Oxford could have meant extinction for the club. He was there for the match at home where the fans turned their backs on the team during the lap of honour, the last match of the pre-Munto era.

This one could be different.

Less about the meat and more about the trimmings.

He didn't know what Crumble had planned for the Bentinck protest. Coventry had a decent firm and would be turning out – perhaps, because of their dreadful season, not in the same numbers as could have been expected, but it could be tasty nonetheless. There could be heavy drinking if Bull was in the mood.

All in all, it wasn't a match he would ordinarily take Beef, but this was different.

He was sixteen. He was a man. He could decide what he wanted to do. This could be a rite of passage for him, a step into adulthood.

Do you want to go against Coventry?

Course I do.

You know that there's a protest planned. The conversion of the Bentinck...

...the new Guatemala Joe's?

That's it. It's a famous old pub and a Notts landmark. People aren't happy.

What's the protest involve?

I don't know. All I know is that your uncle is going.

Is he? Wow...if it goes off, he could lose his job.

...and that's not like losing a job in a warehouse.

We'll have to look after him.

We'll behave ourselves.

I'm deffo coming, dad.

Coventry's got some lads, Beef.

So? You're behaving yourself, right? Dad, you're nearly fifty – you shouldn't be talking like this. You should be talking tactics and strategy. You should be moaning in the stands with all the other old gits.

At Notts? There hasn't been any trouble for years.

What about Man City at home? Beefy said, grinning, spearing chips and a chunk of Tikka onto a fork and dipping it into an amalgam of curry sauce before almost guiltily putting it into his mouth. His dad spotted the waitress who may have been Estonian or Lithuanian, and signalled to her. She came over, all tights and black ballerina shoes, a weary look, blonde hair tied back into a chaste ponytail.

Momentarily, lost for words, he pulled himself together and ordered a coke and another Magners. She walked away without the slightest acknowledgement as if the act of adding the script to the notebook was recognition enough.

The East Europeans may be cheap, Beef, but their customer service skills are often bollocks, he said, watching her walk away.

Man City, dad?

That afternoon, after the 1-1 draw, HobNob, Bull, Grandad and Mini-Beefy headed for the car in the Portland car park. Man City fans in front, lots of Notts. Crowded streets. HobNob remembered him. The scrawny tramp outside the Navi, swaying, pissed, not even bothered enough to turn up for the match, drinking in South Bank Forest Central for the duration of it. Oversized car coat straight from a sale rack at a Salford charity shop, a Yankees baseball cap. Gaunt cheeks flushed, scarred.

Come on then, you cunts.

Come and have some. Come on.

On his own, an oscillating beacon, an insecure lighthouse in the midst of a maelstrom, his pint glass, urine-tinted rotgut spilling over the sides.

One punch and he's down.

One punch and he's on the deck.

One little punch.

His two fat mates, the Burberry, Stone island blousons, asking every fucker out.

Who wants it?

You County cunts.

Who wants it?

Walking up to students and shirters.

County cunt. Wanker. Come on then.

A family of Man City fans. Dad, with a Sneinton patois. Ultimate plastic, dad, in a town full of plastics, from Sneinton, supporting Man City. Lots of young Notts lads behind, most of whom look like students or session guitarists for the Stone Roses. He's giving it shit – as are all his kids – Nottingham, all of them, Nottingham – he's giving it the big one, you're the shit of Nottingham, and there's this lad in a blue Stone Island blouson tripping up anyone he can see with a serial killing shit-eating cheddar-teethed smirk and HobNob remembers...

...and he is sure that Bull remembers that they could do fuck all about it.

Fuck all.

A thirteen year old boy to protect

A seventy year old who disapproved of their past, and for who the last decade of relative Bully brotherly peace and quiet has been a process of rebuilding family relationships, an establishment of normality.

In short, they could do nothing.

A low point.

Taking family to the game. Risky. Just like now.

Approaching Fifty, well past Forty.

Retired.

Family men.
But it's still there.
The codes, the rules, the structures. The protocols.
The fists.
Outside the Navi.
The rage within. Hatred of away fans.
Total pathological hatred.
(Fuck them.)
(Man City always do us.)
Hate Man City with an abiding, burning passion.

The new generation of young Notts on the other side of the ground and Clarkson, Paulie, Breaker, Crumble and all the gang were elsewhere.

The students being threatened had looks on their young faces, which suggested that the idea of fighting at football matches was as bizarre as the angular quadratic equations they learned in their studies at Central college.

It was a low point...

Walking past as if it wasn't happening was a low point...

Shameless haunts me even now....hate Man City, Beefster. I couldn't have hit him, could I?

Not really. You did well to walk past. It still goes off...Doncaster...that fat Yorkshire bloke with the bald head underneath the Sirrel tree trying to fight with everyone.

I ought to have planted him, too. Dad was with us...and you...

Those days are over, surely.

I know, son.

What was the worst defeat you ever suffered, dad?

Defeat? On or off the pitch?

Off it, of course. On the pitch...Kettering away in the cup.

That was gruesome...the lowest on pitch moment...247 Notts fans for a cup replay. Apart from a great Jay Smith goal and Mike Edwards trying his best, there was nothing. Nothing. 2-1. The fans...HobNob winced, put down his knife and fork...

Off the pitch, dad? Ever been badly battered?

There was Wigan that Sunday afternoon when we got caught cold. Hartlepool, a couple of others, but the worst was coming back from Gillingham away. No question.

Gillingham?

In Kent ... but it wasn't Gillingham that did us, Beef ... let's go get pudding, and I'll tell you...

The Worst Notts Defeat Ever

Mark Barry: *HobNob told me that his son had asked that question. While he answered it, and there is general agreement of the answer amongst Notts hooligans, rather than continue with his tale, I have a tape recording in my notes for Ultra Violence. Taken in the Navigation after some non-descript home match, it contains a conversation with seven or eight of the lads who attended Gillingham the same day Frank Bruno fought at Wembley Arena in the autumn of 1987. All the lads who took part in the conversation eventually appeared in Ultra Violence. For the sake of diversity, I transcribed the recording in its entirety. Here it is.*

The Navigation Pub
Meadow Lane, Nottingham.

(Talking about an away fixture at Gillingham.)

Clarkson: That pub in Gillingham was one of the filthiest pubs I have ever been in, and it was one of the shittiest grounds. A ramshackle place. Falling to bits. This is the most charitable way you can describe that place. Falling to bits. Spotless today, but back in the eighties? No way. Winding streets, horrible locals. I'd been there a few times, and Colchester, but that was a tough part of the world to visit. Expensive on the train, a long way on the coach. I used to hate it when Gillingham were in the same league as us. That was an away to avoid.

Breaker: We had it with their lads after...

Bull: I remember that. Ten of them, up that street behind the away stand...

Clarkson: We ran them, they scarpered up the top. HobNob ran at some of them, made a big show of it, come on then, come on then and...

Breaker: ...just as he was about to charge, he found his way blocked by a moped parked between two parked cars...

(laughs)

Bull: Typical of him. Always doing daft stuff like that.

Little Dave: I can't remember, like, did they stop and fight when he got going again?

Clarkson: Nah. They were on their toes.

Clifton Tom: When we got back to London, we had a right good booze around Covent Garden. We were fucking steaming.

Little Dave: Always a good trip down to London. Used to love them...

Clifton Tom: Fucking expensive nowadays. Costs a fortune to go on the train to a London match today. It wasn't bad, back in those times. Been some great days out...QPR, Orient...

Haxford: ...Fulham on a Tuesday night, the Freight Rover Trophy...and you two cunts managed to get ejected even with a thousand there, tops...when they were crap...

Bull: It was Norris...he was a bit shit....

(murmurs of mutual agreement)

Clifton Tom: Fifteen pints of lager didn't help your mood, did it?

Clarkson: ...and after, Pompey turned out, about eight. We'd been boozing on and off all day and we were steaming, and on the way to the tube, I don't remember where, but we had just come out of this pub, it was dark, and no one about, a back street pub, and then, from the top of the road, you could hear it...

Narrator: What?

(All look at each other. Towards me. Together...)

All: "6...5...7!"

(laughs)

Clifton Tom: Pompey's mob hanging around town, about fifteen standing at the top in a line. I thought, oh, shit, it's alright running about with Gillingham and that, but this lot...nah, I was shitting it and I was pissed.

Clarkson: I didn't fancy that. Right bunch of them walking towards us. There was about eight of us...

Little Dave: If that, about six, we were outnumbered three to one...

Haxford: Fuck off, Dave, who's counting...

Breaker: And they were between us and the tube station, so there was no point us running off. I thought, we're going to take a beating here, a real battering...

Clarkson: You two cunts (nodding to Bull) wandered up the road, I thought, oh, fucking hell, we're going to have it now...

Bull: ...HobNob got the idea that they weren't after us, and they wanted a natter.

Little Dave: Like the opening story in *Football Factory*...

Breaker: The Coventry one, the ones where they get slashed in London by Chelsea and the Headhunters weren't even after them.

Bull: We thought we were going to get hammered anyway, so we may as well go and try and sort it out...

Haxford: Grovel, more like!

(laughs)

Bull: That's more like it. Pompey turned out to be looking for Palace for some reason, and when they found out we were Notts, they were quite friendly.

Clarkson: One of our few alliances...

Breaker: That and West Brom...

Clifton Tom: I don't trust any of em. There's no such thing as alliances in football. They'd soon batter the fuck out of us down at Fratton Park if we were taking the piss.

Bull: I'm surprised they didn't whack us.

Narrator: One of those unwritten codes maybe?

Haxford: Just stick to writing, you. Let us deal with the clever stuff...

(laughs)

Clarkson: After that, they went their way and we went ours.

Little Dave: Remember that Tottenham fan?

Breaker: Haha, I do. Looked a bit like Keith Harris...

Clifton Tom: Without Orville...

Breaker: Minding his own business, having a quiet pint. HobNob goes up to him and asks him who he supports...

Bull: He's a fucker when he's had a drink...

Clifton Tom: Says you..

(laughs around the table, Bull laughs along)

Breaker: ...and he says, Tottenham, and your brother goes, what's happened to your lads. Bunch of cunts. What's happened to Tottenham? I hear they got ran by Barnet the other week...

Clifton Tom: ...and Orient the week before...

Clarkson: ...and *Sutton Town* in the Cup...

Breaker: And this bloke goes (in a cockney accent), we've been done over by the faccin law. The faccin law have faccin done all our lads, undercover, innit, they've done all our boys...it's on faccin fire down here...

Clarkson: And your kid goes, I understand that, mate, but fucking *Barnet*...

Clifton Tom: I thought Keith Harris was going to blow a fuse...hahaha

Breaker: ...the chap's mush was a picture. He did not expect that...

Clarkson: Like that time we bumped into Wayne Sleep in South Kensington...

Haxford: He was a bit surprised about that...did he buy us all a drink?

Breaker: I think that was Joe Jordan at Fulham...

Bull: Gary Mills bought me and HobNob a pint in Basildon...

Clarkson: After you got thrown out for ruining that minute's silence for Man Utd...

(laughs)

Breaker: And throwing that Mars Bar at the copper's helmet...

Bull: (visibly cringing) I was only young, what, eighty eight?

Clarkson: We finished in there and went over to pick up the train. I remember we played a load of Belgian fitters at pool in that whore's pub in Kings Cross...

Little Dave: Reciting Python sketches to them and telling jokes...

Breaker :...to famously humourless Belgians ... hahaha

Clarkson: Sadly, the mood changed when we got on the train...

Unforgivably, at this point, the tape ran out, but the tale they told me remained in my head, and when I got the chance, I asked Bull about it and taped what he had to say.

Bull: We had tickets for the last train north from St Pancras, the 11pm 125 going to Sheffield, passing through Luton, Kettering, Leicester, Nottingham and Sheffield. We caught it many a time. Sometimes the train was packed, other times empty – mostly football, some theatregoers. This one was half empty. As we walked merrily along the carriages to try and find two tables together, Haxford noticed a part-time copper he knew on the train, a Special Constable, and the Notts mob piled on and sat around him and his friend. Bro and I missed out on the seats nearest the copper, and we sat three tables down. I noticed four blokes sitting on the table next to where Haxford and the lads were sitting. Older than us, not football lads – they looked military to me. Chunky fuckers, muscled up, tattooed forearms. Harringtons and grey trousers and short-sleeved white polo shirts. Real straight types, veterans of Soul nights at Wigan Casino. They'd been somewhere, a night out. I got a bad vibe off them and I noticed them staring at our lads. HobNob, who was sitting opposite, came round and sat next to me, to keep a close eye on them. You have to remember, we were all hammered – fucking steaming – and I can't remember the details accurately, even HobNob can't remember precisely what happened, but our lads started talking to them. They said they were Hearts fans and had travelled down from Edinburgh to see the Bruno fight. I wasn't part of this, so I have no idea what was said, but the next minute, about five minutes after the train disembarked, all fucking hell let loose.

And they hammered us. They whacked us all over the shop. I'm not kidding; they kicked the crap out of us, Mark. All over the carriage. I realised we were out of our depth. These weren't football lads. These were gangsters, ex-Army, and they were hyped up from the boxing. Haxford managed to escape, but Clarkson and Little Dave got a right beating. I think Dave was stamped and got a couple of broken ribs. Clarkson's eye was a right mess – at least he tried to stand up to them, but the bloke who got it worst was the amateur filth…

Narrator: Who?

Bull: Sorry, the Special Constable.

Narrator: Right, got you.

Bull: That's how I knew they were gangsters. Our kid said they were evolved hooligans, not Hearts at all, you know, the blokes who left football behind and moved into guns, or slaves, or drugs, or illegal currency. Hard cunts, my God. You've written about our kid and me. We were just brave and cheeky daft. We've never hurt any fucker in our lives, but these blokes were out to kill us. I mean, bad style. I was out of my depth, and so was my brother.

Narrator: I remember you saying you didn't like fighting outside football.

Bull: True. HobNob was a pub fighter, really. Night clubs, streets and pubs. Me, I liked it in the stadiums and just outside. These Jocks were anywhere fighters. Ultra violent. Total head cases. The Special...

Narrator: What happened to him?

Bull: You don't really want to know.

Narrator: I do.

Bull: We had been proper rumbled by this point, ran all over, and we were at the top of the carriage. I watched it all happen through the window. Clarkson was getting a kicking. Little Dave was being kicked to fuck under a table. Breaker was taking punches, but all of that paled when I saw what happened to the Special.

Narrator: What happened?

Bull: This silver-haired geezer got up and stamped on his head. He climbed onto the table and stamped on his head. In leather brogues. It was horrible to see. About crushed his skull. I should have helped him. It was attempted murder, that's all it was.

Narrator: What did you do?

Bull: I did what any sane fucker would do and hid in the bogs. Also, HobNob.

Narrator: Oh.

Bull: Not what you want to hear is it, in a book about fearless football hooligans?

Narrator: It's not what I expected.

Bull: I'm haunted by it, to be honest. I should have helped him, but I'd have been battered as well. This Special...I didn't know him. I'd never seen him. I've heard he never went to another game of football, and he left Nottingham. I wish I had more bottle. I was drunk, slow, scared, and I knew full well I was out of my depth. You had the Jock element also...

Narrator: The Jock element...

Bull: These Hearts cunts *hated* the English. I wondered what the vibe I was getting off them was, and it was only when I heard Silverback speak that the penny dropped. The Sweaty genuinely detested the amateur filth for being English. Two strikes on him: Filth and a citizen of the Green and Pleasant. He didn't stand a chance. That was a stamp of loathing. There was no doubt in my mind that he wanted to kill him. No doubt at all. I've been involved in fighting since I was fourteen and I've been watching punch-ups around town since God knows when – Notts is a bloody violent place – but that was the closest thing I saw to attempted manslaughter. Never seen anything like it. I can picture him getting up from his seat in his white polo shirt and black trousers, and jumping up on the table in front of the copper like some northern soul Gibbon. I can still picture him stamping on the fella's head. Fuck off leather brogues. He didn't just stamp on him. The Jock cunt gave him a Blakey's Kiss.

Narrator: Lost you there…

Bull: Your generation don't wear bloody shoes! Blakeys are metal heel protectors, mate. Fix them to the vulnerable spots on your heel with a hammer. Adds six months to shoe life.

Narrator: Thanks for that. I think I can guess what happened next…

Bull: The impact climaxed not with his sole, but with his *heel* and that leather heel was full of Blakey segs. Remember those? Every time the heel made contact, it left a bloody trench in his forehead. That cunt went in for the kill. Silver-haired jock, built like a prop forward. Full of ale, but mostly he was full of hatred. He might have blamed the ale in the morning, in front of the beak, but it was much more than that. Hatred of the English. They *were disgusted by* us. I ain't kidding. Never understood loathing like that before I saw those Jocks. After, I felt I could pass an exam in Understanding Hatred. It was in their eyes. All of them. I've never spoken to a Scottish cunt since, not unless I'm paid to. I work with a Jock on the power stations, and I'm civil to him, but after work, no chance.

Narrator: What if Murray won Wimbledon?

Bull: Who?

Narrator: Andy Murray. Top quality tennis player. Jock.

Bull: Not interested in tennis – a cunts pastime – but to be honest, I would probably cheer whoever he was playing.

Narrator: But he's British….

Bull: Are you taking the piss? He's *Scottish,* and they *all* hate us. They pretend to be mates, they pretend to be

British, but peel back the onion and there's a hatezombie in there. Same as the Taffs. Just as bad. I know a pair of sparks from Derby who got battered in Pontypridd one night. The local Leeks lured them into a false sense of security, allowed them to sit round their bar, shared a few pints with them, had a bite to eat, a few jokes, a few manly guffaws and an earnest natter about the prospects for Cardiff City, but outside in the car park, they let them have it. Annihilated them. Made a right three-phase mess. One of the blokes can't hold his tools properly any more – lost the use of his left hand because one of the Welsh cunts stamped on it and broke every connecting bone in there. Every single one of them. Makes me mad thinking about it. Britain? The 1707 Act of Union? It's a fucking myth.

Narrator: Nice one on the date.

Bull: HobNob mentioned it the other night.

Narrator: I can't get my head round all this violence. All this hatred. I don't mix in these circles…

Bull: Well, you're learning. Doesn't all this annoy you?

Narrator: It makes me angry. It makes me want revenge.

Bull: I'm glad. It should do. The English are fucking hated, you know that, but I never knew *just how much* until I saw the eyes of that sweaty on that train. Jocks? Cunts. I wouldn't piss on one if he were on fire. I'd probably steal his battered Bounty and munch it while I watched him burn, the thick cowardly cunts.

Narrator: What happened to the Special?

Bull: Proper bolloxed. A proper state. Plasma was everywhere, all over the table and train windows. Fluids trickling from his ears. Battered eye sockets, gavelled forehead from where Silvermane's heel connected with his skull. They stretchered him to Luton hospital, tubes sprouting everywhere, passengers looking on, a bemused audience of shocked and tearful faces. Geezer looked like Pinhead out of *Hellraiser*. We heard a few weeks later that he had suffered a fractured skull and a detached retina. Unconscious for three days and the sawbones were worried he would never recover.

Narrator: Bad. Really bad. Any other casualties?

Bull: Apart from a few egos and black eyes, Clarkson and Little Dave found themselves in Luton and Dunstable, then spent the night on the floor of Luton gaol. They took a proper kicking.

Narrator: I cannot believe this. On a Saturday night in England? It's like something out of a horror film. My publisher would hound me out of the office if I presented this as fiction. It's just…just…you can't suspend disbelief here…

Bull: This is kosher, mate. It wasn't just hoolies involved either. In the same carriage as us was a foursome of young lovers from Market Harborough sitting just behind me. Lovely people. Professionals, liberals. Handsome people, a normal hardworking quartet of theatregoers who had just enjoyed a splendid evening watching *Starlight Express*. Picture them if you will, indulging in gentle kisses, walking through Covent Garden, hand-in-hand, after a bite to eat in The Strand, young lovers with music in their ears then, bang, out of the blue, Hell appears on a 125. One of the women was screaming. Young bird with a perm, quite pretty, nice boobs. Screaming the carriage down. That lot will never again catch the last train to Notts. Any night train for that matter.

Narrator: Don't blame them. I don't think I would.

Bull: After, transport Plod crawled all over the carriages looking for stray Jocks and Notts hoolies. The evil cunts from Scotland got lifted straight away. Our lot, a bit more with it, seeing them coming, hid under tables, in toilet compartments, anywhere. Breaker, using his initiative, jumped off the train, hid behind a trolley full of Sunday newspapers and sneaked back on just as the coppers alighted. Those jocks weren't football lads. The fact they follow Hearts is incidental. There was no running about or showing off the old Tacchini symbol while making scary hand gestures. They went straight for the kill. And to this day, no one knows what was said to spark them off.

Narrator: The Boxing….

Bull: Yep, the Jocks had witnessed a full card of boxing at Wembley Arena, including big Frank at his finest. On the ale all day: It wouldn't have taken much to spark them off.

Someone definitely said something, but it was probably innocuous. Well, harmless to you and I. These lads needed it. They *craved* it. They wanted it bad, and we were the unlucky cunts who provided their evening's post-Bruno entertainment.

Narrator: Do you feel that you let the lads down?

Bull: I do. After all these years. It was definitely the worst ever Notts defeat. We ran from Wigan outside the old Springfield Park ground, the one with the grass bank for an away pen, but that was more because of the element of surprise and we were outnumbered three to one in the dark. With Wigan, I guess there were mitigating circumstances ... anyway; I'm getting pissed off with this. It's far too negative ... can we talk about something else? I feel an overwhelming compulsion to smash up a Proclaimers CD and squash a box of tartan shortbread.

Narrator: What about the prospects for Notts in the upcoming season?

Bull: Can we talk about Hearts again?

(laughs)

7. Zero Hour Contract

HobNob called me the Wednesday before the demonstration. He called from his lodgings, and I could hear music in the background. I didn't recognise the music, and I didn't ask what it was. This was only the second call he had ever made to me, and I'm not sure why he made contact. I think he wanted to practice on his new mobile phone, an item of which he was proud and as such, spent a good ten minutes talking about.

E-mail. Internet surfing. Pop3 mailboxes. Differential Wi-Fi connectivity. Skype. The Racing Post app.

He was talking with wide-eyed wonder, like an alien who had recently parachuted down to earth from Pluto. Like many near fifty year old men, technology we take for granted had passed him by. I had just got out of the bath when I spoke to him. I asked him how his job interview had gone...

Not good. No. Not brilliant.

What happened?

I got the job, he said.

I was taken aback, not quite sure whether he was taking the piss.

That's great news, I replied, after a momentary, but noticeable, gap. Why aren't you happy about that?

Turned it down, Mark.

Really?

Yeh. It's okay saying they offered me a job, but actually, they didn't. What they offered me was a zero hours contract. I mean, fuck off.

What's one of those?

What? A zero hours contract?

Yep.

They are horrible. Fucking horrible. It's eerie, he said. I cannot believe those things aren't illegal. Thatcher tried to encourage those back in the dark ages, and she was laughed out of office. We're talking about Maggie Thatcher. Not even the wickedest woman Britain has ever seen could get a zero hours contract White Paper into law. Zero hours. You don't know what that is?

No, I said. Tell me what they offered you…

I reached for my pen and notepad. This was news to me. Since University, I had never had a paid job. I had always written. I did not intend to take a job and thus, the world of work and its vagaries were nothing to do with me. I had never heard of such a contract – another example of media suppression of anything perceived as being opposite the Tory agenda.

Here's a zero hours contract in a nutshell, he said. Fancy a job? Sign on the dotted line. Welcome aboard. Report for your induction on Monday at ten. Hours? Haha. Sorry, you've been misinformed. There ARE no hours! If we need you, we'll call. If we don't need you, we won't. Sit by the phone. Sick pay? Are you having a giraffe? There's no sick pay, no holiday pay, no perks. Nothing. Just think of that glorious feeling of euphoria – you have a JOB!!

Zero Hours Contracts! Minimum wage, no perks and NO GUARANTEED HOURS. What is all that about?

It sounds crazy, I replied. It sounds like madness. What kind of job has no hours?

The kids think it's normal. They're glad to have a job on their CV. If someone buys your book and they are a manager who actually dishes out these zero hours contracts, then give them their money back and call them a cunt.

Haha. I will do.

How did these contracts materialise? When? And do you know what? With some of the companies who offer zero hours, you can't get another job. Take the Pound Goblin. The Pound Goblin offers 25 hour per week and THEN CHANGES THE SHIFT PATTERN EVERY SUNDAY! Ergo? You can't feasibly work another job! I don't know why I'm kicking the shit out of the Pound Goblin: All of retail is this bad. Social care, too. Now my industry's adopting zeros. Sessional work. Self-employed. No employer wants to fork out for holiday pay or sick. All the big DIY chains do that Sunday thing. Every Sunday they mix it up. Can't take another job, so you can't live. No wonder the suicide index is on the rise: The workers are throwing themselves off every available bridge.

Zero Hours Contracts.

Rather than take down the entire contents of his rant, I put the three words in the centre of a spider's web and key concepts emerged on stalks. There was plenty of material to build the web – HobNob was off on one.

And what if you get sick? He commented. It's anti-social. I was on the bus into Notts last week to have a look for phones. Bloke behind me, snorting, snotting, sneezing like a good 'un. All over my neck and shoulders. I turned round to have a word, and he's got a pair of overalls on. You know them card shops? Greetings cards? **The Emporium of Good Wishes.** Such a nice name, such a shit company. Fella had to go to work with flu because they don't do sick pay. Uncivilised. Truck shops are back. Madness. Down to Cameron and Osborne, the satanic Morecambe and Wise of British politics.

I can't come into work, Guv'nor as I have bubonic plague and my mush is one big suppurating pit of exploding pus.

Well, if you don't come in, I'll give your zero hours job to Mustapha.

Okay, then, I'll struggle in. Might be five minutes late.

It's fucking anti-social. Say you're a customer going in to the shop to buy a birthday card for your niece, Cecilia Spark. Some buying experience THAT is going to be, the terrified, starving, flu-ridden staff, germ-infected hands on the gift wrapping, lumpy, emerald slime, litres of translucent sputum dripping all over the verse. Ne'er mind, it's cheap. Some of them cards are EIGHT pence! I remember when cards were three quid! Throwaway society. I mean fuck off.

They're cutting their most expensive cost, I said. Because no one votes, they can do whatever they want. Clever.

The Evil Wizards Have Assumed Control, he replied, somewhat wistfully.

The Evil Wizards? Do you mean lizards? I asked, mindful of David Icke.

Nah, Wizards. A zero hours contract is the ultimate instrument of social control, mate. Keep people low.

Remove the methods by which they can rise. Make them minions. Give a worker money and he or she can make decisions. Starve them of money and they are just a rat pressing a lever in order to survive.

A rat, I said, drawing a rat on my spider's web.

Or a dog. Psychologist called Martin Seligman, right. Nineteen seventy four. Figured depression was connected to a lack of choice, a sense of inevitability. He called the condition Learned Helplessness.

To prove his hypothesis, Seligman invited a beautiful round-eyed German Shepherd called Rosie, into his laboratory. In the centre of which, surrounded by monitors, dials, screens, switches, test tubes and Bunsen burners, was a box the size of a kid's play pen. Half of the box was painted black; the other half was painted white. There was a mezzanine grid for flooring, which as it transpires, was electrified and connected to a 240 volts supply. In the black half was a dog bowl full of Rosie's favourite treat. In she went. She fell on the treat and started munching. Seligman, a top psychologist – who nowadays is a guru for positive thinking and happy-clappy psychology – flicked a switch. Electrified the black half of the grid.

Sparks flew.

Rosie yelped, jumped a foot in the air and scampered over to the white half to safety. Seligman waited a bit and served up more treats in the black half. Rosie, unsure whether the shock was a one off, tentatively wandered over there for more food.

Whoops.

Bad move.

Seligman waited until the dog was slobbering into her bowl and then he flicked a switch, a 240 volt main course. Naturally, Rosie learned quickly that the black half meant pain and no amount of food could persuade her to cross over into the void. Then, nice Mr Seligman, the top psychologist, reversed the schedule.

This time, he electrified the white half.

Rosie, desperate to escape, jumped into the black half, now inert. Confused, trembling, whimpering, Rosie laid down in the black half, clearly scared of the white half. Seligman reverses the procedure one more time.

And then he does it again.

Rosie the German Shepherd learned that no area of the experimental apparatus was safe. Black or white. There was nowhere she could go to avoid being shocked. She laid down in the centre of the box and took all Seligman's shocks, which the nice psychologist continued to administer to gather data. Rosie learned that helplessness is the only solution. She learned that there was nothing she could do.

That's a nice experiment, I said. Nice person.

And the papers call us hooligans evil. This guy writes books on personal development.

I'll have to look him up. Happy-clappy psychologist, you say?

He's fucking vile, but he proved his point. We've all learned to be helpless. The French wouldn't have this zero hours contract shit for ten seconds. They'd be on the streets. They'd be incinerating parked cars and playing tear gas tennis with the Gendarmerie. England? A whole lotta Rosies. That's what we are. A load of shocked dogs. The Tories can do what they want to us because we believe we are helpless. If everyone stopped going to work for one week – I mean, *everyone,* not just one occupational group – the country would tip into economic meltdown and the Tories would stop what they are doing. Zero hours fucking contracts…I cannot believe it…

I put my pad away. Decided to change the subject.

Bull said you went on a date.

Did he now? The tell tale.

He mentioned it in passing.

Yeh, it went well. Naomi; I used to go out with her. We got on well. I asked her out. Yeh, it was a good night. Going out with her on Sunday. You going to the demo?

I am, yes.

Good. I was considering asking Naomi to come down, but…well…you know.

What?

It's like, she's…a girl.

I laughed. Plenty of girls go to football nowadays.

I know, I know. I'll take her next year. She's a nice girl. We get on, and I think she quite likes me, too. I don't know why we split up in the first place.

I guess you were young.

Guess I was. I liked her. She was nice, and I don't meet many nice girls, what with…well…you know, the life I've led.

I saw an inroad.

It flashed at me like the lamp on the nose of an oncoming steam train. It would be an opportunity I would regret missing out on for the rest of my life if I didn't take it. He had softened. He had started to share. What was I? A writer or a hack. Mixing metaphors in my head like a fourth year English pupil after too much Coca-Cola, I took the bull by the horns and jumped into the chink of light with both feet. Knowing full well the risk I was taking with his volatility, I decided to ask him the question. It was probably a stupid thing to do, but I realised that I may never get the chance to be this *intimate* with HobNob Bully.

The question had bugged me for weeks. If he stopped talking to me then…well…I would kick myself forever.

HobNob, can I ask you a question?

Sure. What do you want to know…he said, and I thought his reply was lighthearted.

What was Cedar Forest all about? Your brother won't tell me.

Silence.

A crackle on the phone louder than the hush.

Silence.

Outside, a sparrow perched on my windowsill and pecked at something. I could see his black eyes blink.

More silence.

Nausea overwhelmed me like a stinking blanket. My bowels constricted, and I felt my stomach start to wobble. The fluid in my brain froze.

Shit.

He didn't respond.

I knew then that I had made a huge mistake.

Stillness on the other end of the phone. I wanted whoever was in charge of these things – Fate, God, Destiny, Buddha, Allah or Mother Earth – to swallow me up. I was dying a slow death and then...

Cedars? Nah, it's nothing, mate. Third time I've been in. Not worth talking about.

Is it? I asked, compounding my perceived error...and then, he went straight in.

Identity, mate. I struggle with who I am. Usual fantasy and reality shit. All this shit ... you know ... all this *stuff.* All this identity stuff. Who am I, and that.

What? I asked, like a rubbernecker unable to take his eyes off a five car pileup as he travelled past on the bus.

All this football shit. All this jibba jabba. It's ... well ... you know ... you're a writer. You must understand identity ... the way it works ... the fragmentation ... the *multiplicity* of it ... the fact you can *invent* stuff ... you can *be whoever you want* ... whenever ...

In what sense?

There was a renewed silence. He was thinking, I could tell. I felt he was ready to talk to me. I had made a breakthrough. I reached for my pencil, twirled it.

Waited for him to continue. He did so.

You know. *Identity crises* ... you invent characters ... do you ever *become* them?

No, I ...

... you have to remember who you are in the end ... otherwise ...

... otherwise what, HobNob?

... the Pixies ... you know, the *Pixies* ... little red Pixies with big teeth and wings ... you know ... gossamer wings, like flies ... you must see Pixies?

The Pixies? I replied, open mouthed. Flies?

Or it might have been my fucking *drink* problem you nosy cunt ... he shouted, laughing loudly. Or they locked me up because I discovered the crock of fairy gold at the end of the rainbow! Pixies! Haha. As if I'm going to tell a *writer,* of all people, my personal business! You'll tell every fucker! Haha. Bull said you'd been sniffing about ...

Sorry. I was just curious, I replied, completely embarrassed.

Don't apologise...no need. Anyway, back to business. Did Bull ever tell you about Peterborough...?

I had partially succeeded, but I knew him well enough to know enough was enough. I joined in with the subject change...

Peterborough? At home...he might have done...tell me...

Vikings

HobNob: *I'm glad he did. This was a fucker of a night. Half of me is proud of us, the other half thinks it's madness. Mind you, I don't like Peterborough. I never did before, and I don't now. We could be playing them next year. Things were terrible for me that year. 97. One of the worst years of my life. Everything had gone badly wrong and I'd not attended for much of the season. Judas was in charge. I'd not seen Bull for months – we'd had a big fall out – and this meant Peterborough at home was an important clash for more than one reason...*

29 November 1997
Notts County 2 Peterborough 2

It had been a mild winter and the country bathed in the jubilant afterglow of the victory of New Labour. Six months down the line, the event remained a font of optimism for everyone after the year zero politics of Margaret Thatcher had left the majority of the British population miserable and bereft.

And skint.

The only mitherers? A tiny coterie of multi-millionaire bankers who might have to pay a bit more tax. Certainly, the northern half of the country celebrated and would celebrate onward – the country would surely never re-elect a Tory government and that was cause for a party that would never stop.

November.

A month to go until Christmas, and mild, the Indian Summer lingered. HobNob wore a dark blue Lacoste polo and jeans as he walked up London Road.

London Road is essentially a bridge, an extended bridge between the City and prosperous Rushcliffe, and below to his left, canal people fished – they always would, wearing polo necked Fisherman's jumpers and waterpoofs.

They wore clothes like this whatever the weather and they were creatures of habit.

A lunatic could explode a thermo-nuclear device secreted in a Sherwood garage, thus levelling the entire City and killing everything living for ten miles around and within weeks, the canal fishermen would be back, emerging from their subterranean enclaves into the surreal rainbow glow, ready to dangle their rod and lines into the irradiated morass.

Each one wearing a warm jumper, a thick green coat and a pair of waders.

In the distance, Eastcroft Recycling Station emitted its noxious gases into the atmosphere, tinting the midday sky with a shimmering indigo tinge as if an alchemist had boiled a million blackberries just to witness the emergent spectrum. HobNob noticed the stench – sulphur mostly, a hellish concoction. Citizens wandered the streets of Nottingham as they once did the villages around Bhopal, oblivious to the chemicals that the incinerator plant generated and expelled into the gunmetal skies of a British winter.

But the people of Nottingham noticed the smell.

They tolerated it, turned a blind eye or blamed the Council. Or the drains.

The drains were the scapegoat for everything, HobNob thought.

He looked up and saw the giant Kop stand, and the sight of the old Cathedral filled him with quiet contentment as if in five short minutes, he would be home.

That day's visitors to Meadow Lane were Peterborough. Second in the table behind Lincoln City and two places above Notts. About 2,000 Posh had been tipped to turn up. HobNob remembered the first time he saw Notts play Posh. 1971. He was seven; small enough to be thrown over his dad's shoulder for a piggy back. Six nil. Tony Hateley hat trick, the sights and sounds of Meadow Lane staying with him forever, instantly addictive, the cheering, the rattles, the black and white scarves, the fearsome chants, the unbridled joy and the crowd surges every time Hateley – the natural successor to Tommy Lawton – nodded one into the back of the net. HobNob fell in love with Notts there and then, a lifelong love affair. Football no longer grabbed him – the reality of following Notts' activities on the pitch much less glamorous than he imagined as a child – but he turned out.

He cared.

Would always care. Thousands didn't.

He'd heard that trouble was expected and that Notts were turning out, but it had been five years since he'd been involved. It was nothing to do with him. The coppers had scared him after Luton and besides, his life outside football had been a complete nightmare. Women. Kids. A dream shattered. Lost jobs. A lost house. More crime. More madness. Drink: The usual early middle-aged geezer's nervous breakdown festival.

His dad called it a mid-life crisis, but HobNob knew it was all just another series of nodes in a continuous stream of crazy data, an infinite, flowing river, which commences with a stolen glance between a man and a woman and ends in a terracotta pot of blackened ash.

But it felt bad.

It felt like shit.

Times like that, as much as he loved Notts, as much as they were part of his family, there was no way that he could attend. His life had been going downhill for ages and Notts became a shadow and shadows aren't real.

He saw him standing outside the Norfolk on the other side of the road.

He felt his heart freeze and his parched mouth dry. They had not spoken at all under Blair, and the phone call had come out of the blue.

He saw him.

Blue blouson jeans. Gazelle trainers. Reading a paper, his pint on the floor. Around him, twenty odd Posh and a few Notts.

HobNob stopped, looked around and crossed the busy road at the first opportunity.

Brothers.

The worst fall outs.

The very worst.

Cain and Abel.

His brother had called him and asked him to come to the Posh game. Out of the blue.

HobNob said yes.

It was all *his* fault.

All the bollocks he caused. All the damage he inflicted like a nuclear blast, all the fallout. Part of him thought he would never speak to Bull again, but here they were about to shake hands outside the old Norfolk Inn. He looked well. A lot better than HobNob felt.

Bull, he said, offering his hand.
Cunt, Bull said, smiling, taking it. You look like shit.
It's been tough. How are you?
Not bad. Pint?
Lager. I'll wait here.

HobNob watched his brother merge into the crowd and a memory assailed him for no apparent reason. When it got bad eight months ago, he found himself on the streets with a rucsac full of tee shirts and a bag of toiletries. In a Mapperley pub, hammered, skint, desperate, he asked one of the Notts lot, a minor figure, but someone he had shared time with, someone he knew, whether he could kip on his sofa.
Just for one night.
Otherwise, it was the streets.
The fella said no.
His expression eloquent.
As if he knew that by denying a kindness, he would be inflicting misery.
HobNob shrugged his shoulders, guzzled his pint, threw his rucsac over his shoulder and walked out of the pub. That was one of the lowest points.
You don't get much lower than that in football.
That night, he slept underneath the Mapperley War Memorial and all the romance about the brotherhood of Notts fans dissipated like the early morning fog.

Bull emerged from the crowd with two pints. The crowd parted easily in front of him. He passed over the pint and HobNob downed half of it in one.
It won't run away, you know, Bull said.
Thirsty.
I've heard you've been thirsty quite a bit just lately.
You heard right. How you been?
Up and down. Work's going alright. Coming down here much?
No. You?
Not much. What do you reckon to Fat Sam?

Jury's out as far as I'm concerned, but fourth in the table isn't that bad, HobNob replied, pouring back the rest of the pint. Many Peterborough in there?

Nah. On my way down from the station, I saw tons on the way into town.

Big day out for them. Many in the Bentinck?

Quite a few.

Cunts team. Posh. Not cockneys. Not carrot crunchers. Hybrids.

As they spoke, two young Peterborough fans turned to look, having heard the conversation. They would have seen someone twice their size standing next to someone else with eyes as black as an unlucky cat's coat. They pretended to be looking at a point behind the brothers, perhaps the ramshackle pine warehouse or the equally dilapidated Greyhound Inn in the distance.

Have a feeling there'll be action today, Bull said.

Up for it?

Nah. I've just landed this decent job and anyway, Jessica has me under orders. Have to be back for ten, he replied, a subtly guilty look that only another ex-football hooligan would recognise.

A look that meant two things – those days are over and I'm under the thumb.

Bull lived and worked near Skipton and had met a girl up there. He seemed happy the last time HobNob spoke to him.

The two men spoke about family business over another pint, but not once did they talk about the thing that caused the row, which at the beginning of the day, was a good plan.

They finished the pints and took a walk down to the Aviary on the bridge. On their way, they saw little gangs of Peterborough – in the gear, casuals, lads, looking for it, on the fringes of the Meadows – walking down towards the Kop. Stopping for a few in the Greyhound. Both of them noticed there were no Notts about or no Notts lads anyway. Both of them without saying anything felt detached and disconnected. The Luton warning had worked for both of them, and they were both getting old.

HobNob looked at his brother.

See them cunts over there? He pointed to fifteen Peterborough outside the Greyhound, typical lads on the lookout. No singing, no chanting, just staring and drinking – like a pack of wolves waiting for deer to walk past their lair.

I do.

We'd have steamed into them at one point. HobNob began to feel slightly irritated. They've taken over our patch.

I know. None of our business, brother.

Yeh, I know. I can do without another…

…where are the lads?

They're all getting old. Haven't you heard? It's a nicer country because New Labour is in power. No one brawls at matches anymore.

Bull grinned slightly and nodded as the Peterborough lads faded from view.

Someone should have told these hybrids that, he said, as they crossed the roundabout next to the Boots Social Club.

It was the same scenario in the Aviary on the bridge.

The two of them stood quietly outside. Despite four bouncers, three hundred lads stood on the terrace, and they were all Peterborough. They could be seen streaming across the bridge. They drank in Cheers and the TBI, and here they were singing outside the Aviary on a mild November day. The Bully brothers, surrounded by them, and seemingly the only two Notts fans in there, put down their pints, went to the bar.

Bull ordered four cans of Red Stripe. They cracked open one each and parked the other two as they watched the hordes of Peterborough on their big city day out. Mansfield, Lincoln and Grimsby were three other teams who regularly exported thousands to Nottingham on a Saturday and at one time, there would be fighting the length and the breadth of London Road, but now it was all Peterborough.

Forest were away. There hadn't been much action over there lately.

It seemed that Nottingham had grown up.

A Peterborough fan, who looked a little like the lead singer out of Department S only with much redder hair, leaned over and pointed at HobNob's drink.

That's brewed near me, that.

What? Red Stripe? He replied, tilting his can.

Yeh. That.

Where's that?

Bedford.

I thought it was brewed in Kingston, Jamaica?

That's the good stuff. They brew that shit under licence. Bedford.

I thought this didn't taste like the stuff when I first drank it.

Definitely not. You Notts? Department S asked.

Yep, HobNob replied, not feeling any immediate threat as the man was smiling and smelled as if he was going out on the pull when he arrived back in Peterborough. Bull looked on impassively, taking a giant gulp. HobNob knew that he hated away fans and despite his protestations, he could see his eyes, and they weren't eyes that cared much about his wife and his new job.

Where are all your lads?

No idea, mate. Try the Navigation.

Been there. Coppers wouldn't let us in.

That's where the lads are.

Thousands of us here today. We've been all over the country. Thousands of us.

Oh, good, HobNob said, but thinking something else entirely inside.

The bloke began to talk about how good Peterborough's away following had been that season, and he talked until Bull finished his can and signalled to HobNob without referring to Department S in any shape or form.

Mid-sentence, the brothers walked off, leaving their interlocutor to his masturbatory fantasies of global Blue domination.

As they walked out, past the now-singing Peterborough on the terrace, hundreds of them, HobNob watched Bull's expression change a little more.

Jesus, how could you listen to that shit? I should have planted him.

He was being friendly.

He was being a cunt. Navi! He ordered. I'm on the Vodka. I mean...*look at them*...

There was a sea of blue, punctuated with an absence of black and white. Embarrassing. Notts had been relegated to the bottom tier for the first time in years, and the Saturday crowd had dropped dramatically. Although Allardyce had strung a few wins together, the football was gruesome to watch as it had been at Bloomfield Road in his last management job. An unpleasant man, an unpleasant footballer and an unpleasant manager.

However, Derek Pavis, the Chairman, had predicted a decent gate for this top of the table clash in the Post, and he would be gutted if the "Nottingham Public", as he described them, didn't attend.

Early doors, it looked as if Joe had ignored his pleas.

On the short journey from the Aviary to the Navigation, via Turney's Quay (the bridge, the brook, the houses, so fragile they wouldn't withstand a tempest), eight Peterborough lads began to follow them.

With large numbers of people about, this could have been a coincidence, but it seemed to both Bully brothers that they were being followed.

The pack behind seemed aware that the brothers were Notts as if the pair of them were wearing black and white bobble hats. The Peterborough gave an impression: Lots of blue jumpers, half-length wool coats and denim jackets. Jeans, smart Adidas and Nike trainers. Curly hair and longish wedges. Peterborough trendies who had enjoyed, it seemed, plenty of ale.

The impression they were being followed was amplified when the brothers turned into Turney's Quay and the eight men, instead of continuing down London Road to the Kop, turned the same way. Into Turney's Quay.

The brothers tensed. Metaphorically, they were on the clock. The twin bells mounted on the clock primed to chime.

Ring. Ring. Ring. Ring.
Eight versus two.
Ring. Ring. Ring. Ring.
No assistance in sight.
The old odds, but ten years later.
(Ten years older)
(Retirement)
(A well-earned retirement)

As they walked, the Peterborough conversed as a gang, the sentences coming from everywhere and addressed to no one in particular, an ensemble, like a barbershop octet.

All they needed were the straw boaters.

They articulated their Snakebite opinions loud enough for the brothers to hear, and their comments about Notts County – delivered in that curious, crossbreed cockney/rustic accent, as if Alf Garnett had married the daughter of Thomas Hardy – weren't pleasant. They certainly hadn't come to Meadow Lane to pay homage to the oldest football team in the world.

Wankers team ... no lads ... little club ... wankers ... no lads ... shit town ... I hate Nottingham ... we'll hammer these ... tossers ... little club ... wankers ... we're too big for this league ... wankers ... shit ground ... we'll batter the cants after ... where are they ... little club ... wankers ...

If they wanted to jump the brothers, it would have been easy. A cul-de-sac, much like TV's *Brookside*. Full of parked cars and neat balconies – when taken together, almost a verandarium. Pacific, serene. No coppers. Inside the houses, civilians enjoyed their weekend pointedly ignoring the activity about to start not a hundred yards behind them in one of the league's best stadia.

Young couples enjoying an afternoon in bed.

Students watching *The A-Team* in an ironic fashion.

Mums spending hours on the phone lamenting varicose veins, their lack of sex, putting their offspring's literacy and numeracy down to bad teachers.

Fathers watching the Hennessy Gold Cup.

No one would see.

No one would watch the massacre through double-glazed windows.

No one would be aware.

No one would witness, and no one would mop up the blood.

Faccing cants ... We'll take these ... batter em outside ... little club ... shit nightlife ... I mean, what happened *to Nottingham, huh? .. .cants cants cants cants...*

HobNob felt his muscles tauten. It seemed unnaturally silent; the only sound the macho wittering coming from the hybrids behind. He could see Bull's fists clench, on edge, ready, but both of them carried on walking as if nothing was happening. The barbershop octet was right on their heels and chattering away. Within punching distance, a long limb, a boxer's limb, an Adder stiffening...one of them...

Five nil ... the Posh are going up ... little cants ... little club ... smash em ... batter em ...

Any minute now, the brothers thought, simultaneously.

Any second now.

Got the time, mate?

(A punch to the back of the head.)

(A trainer in the back.)

(A knife in the ribs?)

Nah, these faccing northern cants ... nah, these cants ... eight nil ... smash em ... what crappy nightlife there is rahnd ere ... crappy beer ... cants ... wankers ...

The two of them expected the works.

The Full Monty.

(A knee bent, passionately driven, crushing a nose, the bollocks.)

(A Milwall Brick.)

(A Blakey's Kiss.)

A cul-de-sac.

Out of the way.

No coppers.

Wired...tense...deep...

They *needed* it...

(Come on. Come on...)

(Come on...)

But it never happened.

They didn't even attempt a trip...the old trick.

Or the time ruse…
Got the time, mate?

Inside the pub, which was bursting with Notts, Bull eventually ordered four pints of lager and four double vodkas.

Pity, that. Bull said.

I know. I know. Brought back memories, huh.

It did. I hate these fuckers.

Yep.

The pub was full, and quite a few people knew the brothers and some of them came over to talk. Not as many as you might think, men being men, and it had been four years since they had been involved.

At the football, you are only as good as your last fight, HobNob said, and the brothers didn't care. They sipped their beer and drank their vodkas in one.

Unfortunately, after a pint and vodka, they made the classic mistake of talking about the recent non-football related past.

It was Bull's fault. He had to say something – it was in him. He had to say something dry, something that needed saying (that HobNob had behaved badly and should apologise to family, which was true), but the problem was, it wasn't the environment, it wasn't the time, and following on from the Peterborough false alarm, the pressure and the tension rose.

HobNob saw Bull's eyes sparkle just like they used to.

The drink. The vodka. The snake brain, the alcohol seeping south, passing the cortex and the civilising consciousness, dripping like a leaking ceiling into the prehistoric parts, the cave dweller's region, the domain of ultra violence, the *killzone*, an area, which on occasion (usually football related), dominated Bull. HobNob had seen his brother's eyes flare like that on many occasions, and he knew what usually followed.

He suspected that the retirement mentality had just left the building.

Just as it seemed that it would all go wrong, that it would all end up in a big family mess and the reunion would be a bad one, perhaps a permanent schism, Bull smiled.

I won eighty quid earlier, he said, his voice slightly slurred, a vodka-influenced subject change. I got off the train, stopped off at the Tote and did our usual thing.

Smash Box?

Three dog. Romford. Smash box.

Ah! Blind?

Deffo. Three dog. A score at seven to two. Fourth favourite. I put the bet on and forgot the price; naturally, it drifts to fours. I checked the SP after the bet. No chance. Slowest dog in the race and just coming back off a trial in which it finished third of three. I started looking for another dog in the next to get my score back. Of course, the three pinged the lids and won a length never headed. Four to one. Let's have another drink.

Suits me.

Bull had noticed that HobNob hadn't been making many trips into his wallet pocket. You skint? He asked.

Well, it's like this...HobNob replied, shrugging his shoulders ironically, a time-worn gesture.

I know, I know, between jobs.

You see. I don't need to tell you.

Well, Bull said. This one is on the Tote.

They had a pint of lager remaining, and it was five to three. The brothers had consumed six pints of lager, two cans of Red Stripe and six single vodkas. It was time for the Southern Comfort, a traditional Arriba drink and something classy to end the lunchtime session. He ordered four doubles with lemonade, no ice, and the barmaid, a brassy Meadows blonde by the name of Nicola, who on her nights off was well known to two or three of the Notts lads, served it up and took the money. Bull passed the two drinks over. The pub was emptying now, the Notts eager to watch the game about to take place not a hundred metre sprint away from the pub. There was space for them to put down the glasses on a circular occasional table by a pillar.

To Notts and to old times, Bull said, raising his glass. HobNob mirrored the gesture and the words.

They downed the Southern Comfort in one.

They drank half a pint of their lager, left the other half and without another word, they walked out into the November sunlight…

2-2

A fantastic game of football marred only by two thousand ranting Posh in the Kop making their presence felt.

The Bully brothers sat in the Fellows after the game. Talking with three hybrids around the same table. One, a short ginger-haired chap wearing an olive green bomber jacket, was holding court to the assemblage.

We've been all over this season, he said. All over. Thousands. We took fifteen hundred to Rochdale, and they shat it. Just like you lot have, no offence. Forty hanging outside that pub on the corner. We ran em all over the North West. They didn't stop running until they reached Manchester. The boys wrecked a pub up there. Not me, mate. I don't do that kind of thing, but we killed it.

Bull sipped his pint. No offence taken, he said.

What? Ginger replied, his two mates next to him, sipping their lager.

You said no offence. I said no offence taken.

Oh, yeh. Right. Rotherham. We expected tons up there, a right ruck. In that Millmoor pub. The Colliers. Them miners. We've had fun up there before, mate, but when we got there, they wouldn't come out the pub. Seriously. Wouldn't come out the pub. Hundred of us, no coppers. They shat it.

We've been there, HobNob said, remembering the High Street battle, but the hybrid shook his head.

Not the same is it, mate, no offence. You've got no lads, he said, gesturing around the pub. I mean, look at this. It's all Posh.

HobNob looked around the Fellows, Morton and Clayton real ale house.

It was indeed, he noticed, full of Peterborough.

There was one in particular that he'd noticed. Six foot seven. Curly hair down to his shoulders. Frame hewn in the gym or on the building site. Denim jacket underneath a leather box coat. Timberland boots. Loud. Very loud. Swigging lager. King of the Pride. The rest were the usual. Skins. Moptops. Wedges. Straights. Curlies. A good hundred of them.

No Notts.

A quiet turnout today, it must be said, HobNob replied quietly.

He looked at his brother surreptitiously. Worried. In the old days, Bull would have dropped the hybrid without a second thought. HobNob would have glassed him in a fit of indignance, but times had changed.

They weren't hooligans now.

They'd moved on.

Retired.

Claiming the Hooligan Pension.

The Hooligan Monday Book.

I've never seen any of your lot, another hybrid piped up. You've never been down London Road.

HobNob and Bull shrugged their shoulders.

Sipped their beer. *What are you thinking, brother?* HobNob thought.

Fuck me, what about Macclesfield, Ginger continued. We *totalled* that ground. One nil and we're on the pitch. Fucking magic that was. What a day out! We took two thousand up there, and there was a standoff outside the away end. Coppers in riot gear. Helmets, tear gas, the lot. It was the bollocks, wasn't it lads, he said.

Both his hybrid friends averred that it was.

The Bully brothers said nothing, the faintest of smiles on their faces.

HobNob remembered one time when his brother took on Grimsby virtually single-handed at Woodall Services. Luton at home. He remembered the suicide walk in Bath. On the main drag outside White Hart Lane. Hartlepool. Mansfield. He remembered the times they'd fought each other, outside the Fountain, the Dog and Bear, the Cross Keys in Arnold, the Grosvenor in Sherwood.

That fuse must be getting longer, he thought.

Ginger carried on.

Swansea brought fifty lads up to London Road, and we battered the living shit out of them. Coming up to Peterborough and taking liberties. And the best of all, Scarborough...

We've been there...HobNob attempted to create a conversation, but Ginger ignored him.

That was the bollocks that was...fuck me...we...

...after a while, it all fused into one.

A Maltloaf conversation. Add currants. Add molasses. Add jam. Add flour. Add almonds and sugar and honey and let it all *blend*....

A Maltloaf hooligan monologue, which opened, transpired and then continued, the Ginger hybrid, no senatorial orator he, squeezing the pip that was Peterborough's upcoming title season for all it was worth. A long diatribe of Cockney egotistical self-regard and the second masturbatory portrait of Peterborough's violent brilliance the brothers had heard that day.

Doncaster, Hull, Hartlepool, Exeter – oh, the riot there! – and Chester on a Tuesday.

Plucky Chester with its city walls, Roodeye racecourse and beautiful women.

Invaded, pillaged, raped and slain by the hybrid Viking hordes from a town surrounded by endless fields of turnips somewhere past Rutland.

HobNob and Bull sat there quietly and waited for the torrent of words to continue.

It soon did.

I mean, you lads. We expected some fun up here. To be honest, we expected some decent opposition. It's built for fucking scrapping, Nottingham. Look at them alleys and cut-throughs on the way to the ground. I thought we'd be ambushed. I mean, this is *Nottingham!* This is a Big City. It's our Big Day Out. I mean, what do you lads say? We're just fucking *yokels!* Well, us yokels been here since ten, and we've not seen you all day. Not a peep. Not a murmur...where were you? We thought you had some lads. Look, we're in your pub, drinking your beer, shagging your women and having a jolly time and your lads are nowhere about.

As I said earlier, it's been a quiet day, HobNob said, aware that the hybrid was in danger of repeating himself.

He was more concerned about his brother.

The glint in the eye as sharp as a razor had just appeared, and Ginger, his two mates and HobNob himself were in potential danger. The odds were insurmountable, and each hybrid had a weapon in his hand, a weapon of convenience.

His brother took a sip of his pint and the danger dissipated. Ginger continued...

The Big City. We expected a lot more. Where are Forest? We always have a do with them. They haven't turned out either...

They're away, Bull replied, coldly, quietly.

Where? One of the other lads asked.

Dunno. Don't care about Forest.

That's a pity; he followed up, his skinhead shining underneath the spotlights above the table. We could have had a good punch-up with them. Unlike you cunts.

The three of them started to guffaw, and it seemed to onlookers that their hilarity was uproarious.

HobNob and Bull sat quietly.

Bull's expression could have signified anything, but the dark sparkle stayed away.

HobNob winked.

That's right, lads. Bit embarrassing for the City, he said.

Banter.

Masculine changing room towel slapping.

Ho. Ho. Ho.

Chat between the victor and the defeated.

Ho. Ho. Ho.

Banter.

(Unlike you cunts.)

Drink, lads? Bull offered, standing, reaching into his wallet.

Nah, it's mine, said one of the hybrids, smirking, dirty blonde, spiked, with a wispy moustache and a green blouson over a polo neck.

Neither Bully brother objected, and the hybrid soon returned with five pints of Stella.

The Fellows is a country-famous pub, which brewed its own real ale, but bar three or four travellers passing the time between trains by reading the newspaper, and the odd stray alcoholic staring into the reflective lens of his own traumatized life, ale drinkers were conspicuous by their absence. Everyone in the pub drank from a tenderly handled pint glass full of lager, which resembled liquefied amber; hooligan communion wine.

The three hybrids started talking amongst themselves.

While sipping his pint, HobNob stared at the giant Peterborough fan with his (much younger) cronies and Bull stared at some fixed point in space. On the streets outside, seen through a murky window in need of attention, he could see it was dark, a winter night, and it was starting to chill. Cars flashed past, heading toward Castle Boulevard, headlights painting their luminous pictures on the door at the entrance to the pub.

Occasionally, a Peterborough supporter would come in, full of the joys of spring.

There wasn't a Notts fan to be seen. With little warning, Bull picked up his pint glass and drained it in one.

Time to go, gents, he said.

Immediately, HobNob followed suit and hands were shaken for no other reason than that was an expected code between drinking men.

The retired hooligan brothers left the pub.

I'm going to fucking KILL them cunts, Bull shouted, booting a Citroen parked illegally outside Redmaynes, putting an elliptical dent in the car door, which would cost a monkey to fix.

His brother shook his head.

No chance, Bull. We're outnumbered. They'll kill us. Notts lost this one.

Fuck off, cunt. You're just as bad. You're a shitter.

What do you mean?

You shat it in there. I hate these cunts. Hate em. Hate em. HATE THEM!

Bull smashed at the door of a martial arts emporium with a boot and two meaty punches. They walked up towards the station, Bull ranting all the way.

I wish I had some backup.

You're not fighting, Bull. Stop it and calm down.

You're shitting it. Listen to you. Look, there's three of them!

Three young Peterborough fans walked past the Carrington chippy.

They're shirters, Bull. You can't hit shirters. Stop it and calm down.

Bull thrust his head into that of his brother's. You are SUCH a shitter. Such a coward. I wish you weren't my brother...I wish I had some proper backup. You're a total cunt. I wish you were fucking DEAD...

All the resentment of the past year came flooding out.

You are a WANKER. This is the last time I ever come to see you. Last time I ever come to Notts...

Bull...

Don't give me BULL, you shitter!!! I'm going to the Bentinck. Now stay here and cry...

Bull had gone in the head, AWOL, roaring, twisted and contorted, his fists clenched like rocks, his giant frame shaking, tears of rage in his eyes as he walked up the road to the Bentinck.

HobNob followed him, watched as he went inside.

The pub was empty strangely, all the Peterborough in town or in the Fellows, and he came back out.

Still here, shitter? I'm going to the station. Meet them on the platform, he said, not looking at his brother, walking straight past. HobNob put his hand on his brother's shoulder firmly, but he shook it off angrily and gave him some more abuse in the middle of the road – taxi drivers from the rank opposite observing quietly, a pair of drunks, two drunken brothers, *kaffirs,* on the ale, the aftermath...

...and he kept on walking underneath the arches at the top of the stairs, a homeless with his Tartan cap begging, a bombed out, fractured, mash-brained presence, scorched and inflamed eyes, mottled, pupils flecked with exploded aquamarine capillaries, pleading, forever pleading, but neither Bully brother saw him or heard him…

…Bull walking down the concourse purposefully, ranting every now and again, HobNob following him, now worried, knowing the platform containing the train to East Anglia was bound to be full of Peterborough and fat, four years out of date, drunk, choleric, frustrated, soft and pathetic, the two of them, old hooligans whose best days were behind them, were…

…about to die and while HobNob didn't care about himself at all, had never done, couldn't care less whether he lived or died, nothing to live for, two broken marriages, maintenance, living in lodgings, carless, jobless, ill, stomach trouble, head trouble, back trouble, bone trouble, double trouble, trouble trouble, a Thatcherite victim, the fucking wicked bitch, one abandoned kid, one estranged, a drink spattered suicide note written in daily parts.

No, he didn't care whether he lived or died, but his brother was a different matter.

He grabbed his brother's shoulder…

Bull, listen…

FUCK OFF, FUCK OFF, FUCK OFF he replied, punching his brother's shoulder, hard.

Come on, man, we're going to die down there. Hundreds of them.

I DON'T FUCKING CARE! Bull screamed, attracting the attention of the British Rail staff and several passengers coming up from the London train, all of who moved swiftly on.

Let's go and get some backup, Bull. Let's go and find Breaker and Clarkson and stuff…come on, we've packed it in…

You shitting CUNT, he said. I don't fucking NEED THEM…

He sprinted down the stairs onto the platform, knowing there would be a hundred Peterborough waiting for the eight twenty five to Norwich. HobNob chased him down.

He knew he was going to die, the pair of them were going to die, and he said a silent prayer as he ran down the stairs...

...into an empty platform.

Bull stood there.

Must have missed them, he said, looking foolish.

Taking aim, coiling, unwinding; he cocked his neck like the hammer of a pistol and headbutted a train timetable three times.

BASTARD! BASTARD! BASTARD!

HobNob was relieved.

Can we go home now, Bull? This is stupid.

No chance, he said. We'll wait for them nobheads to come out of the pub. Now piss off and leave me alone.

I'm not going anywhere.

He sat down on a bench in front of the café. The station was shut, and oddly, there were no passengers about. Deathly silent. HobNob realised that the Peterborough in the Fellows must be coming for the next East Anglia train. He found a timetable poster and had a look – nine twelve. They had about half an hour to get out of there.

He leaned on the café wall and let his heart rate abate. Watched his brother sitting there, seething, on the point of madness. Hoping his brother would calm down in time and see reason.

Talking to him wasn't going to help.

Silly idea.

As he thought about it, it hit him.

HobNob realised that he didn't fancy it anymore.

That he had grown out of it.

That it was 1997 and that it was all over.

He had done the right thing.

Coming today was a mistake and he was going to give that up.

All of it.

Not just the fighting, but the match. Notts.

All of it.

The run down the stairs.

The fear, the adrenalin.
The barren windswept platform (a second chance?).
No more fighting.
He couldn't do it.
The spin dryers. The black eyes. The stamped heads. The bleeding gums. The broken noses. The lamped jaws. The cop wagons. The stinking cop stations, the dirty gaols smelling of old men and old blankets. The puke and the piss on the walls. The appearances in front of the beak. The snide solicitors counting the fees in increments. The beaks themselves, making an example. The lies told to employers.
No more fighting.
He couldn't hack it.
A second chance.

Ten minutes passed in silence on the empty train station and then, Bull stirred.

HobNob went over slowly, almost sneakily, and sat next to him on the bench.

Alright, Bull? He asked.

His brother nodded. Sorry about that, bro. I get so…irritated.

I know you do.

I hate away fans. I fucking hate them. Gobby cunts.

Yep.

Sorry about saying all that, Bull said, not making eye contact, focusing on a train pulling up on Platform 5, an Inter City 125 heading for London St Pancras. You're right, you know. All this is stupid. Our lot don't care so why is it always us? Why us? And who gives a shit. Huh? Who cares…?

We do, HobNob replied. It's just that it's all over.

Fighting?

All of it. The good times. Notts. Scrapping. It's irrelevant. We can't keep scrapping like this. Too much to lose.

I know.

Real life's taken over. I've got my lad to look after, and you've got Jess to think of.

Yep.

Can't keep doing this.

No, you're right, I know. I just get wound up. I'm not coming to football – too much angst...

We'll go and do something else on a Saturday...

Good idea, Bull nodded. Got to do something on a Saturday. Can't stay in with the missus watching Grandstand...

Or worse, going shopping for wallpaper.

Fuck that! Let's go dog racing...

Yeh, and horse racing. It was the Hennessy today.

We could go to Sittingbourne. Crayford, Romford, Newcastle, Hove...

Newmarket, Ascot, Sandown, Hexham ... HobNob continued.

We could go to pictures like we used to.

Nah, HobNob shook his head. Hasn't been anything worth seeing for years...not since...

...*Rita Sue and Bob, Too*...yeh, I know.

Full of ale, moods shifting, they both started to chuckle.

On the platform, two Peterborough shirters, both wearing spectacles, full of beer, talking animatedly, swayed toward the bench.

It had started to turn even colder.

HobNob stood up. Your train isn't for another hour. Let's go to the Bentinck and have a last pint, avoid all these hybrid cunts...

As long as you're on the bell, tightarse, Bull replied, putting his arm around his elder brother as the two of them ambled toward the staircase up to the concourse. HobNob felt a wave of relief. The wave felt a little like sunshine. He had managed to calm down his brother for the only time he could remember, and it felt good.

It felt good to laugh.

Just as they walked onto the empty concourse, the ticket offices to their right, a gang of Peterborough twelve strong, walked straight towards them.

All of them plastered and all of them lads.

Ambling from the concourse entrance to the platforms.

HobNob, bang on the clock, switching gears without knowing why, spotted one of them immediately, a lanky young lad not long out of his teens, six foot five at least.

A black polo neck. A Bravo, hard faced.

Someone who wanted a fight. Someone who needed a fight.

The others were older, roughly the same age as the Bully brothers.

Watch out, Bull, he whispered.

Seen them, his brother replied.

They both carried on walking.

It seemed that the hybrids had stopped talking and started anticipating.

HobNob didn't know whether he was imagining things. He didn't think so. He felt his heart stop and his blood run cold. They were fifteen feet away and coming toward them.

The brothers carried on walking as did the hybrids.

A clash was inevitable, a confluence, an amalgam, a collision.

HobNob froze.

For some reason, the young hybrid in the polo had spotted Bull and was walking straight towards him.

He didn't know why Polo had focused on Bull.

He could just as easily have focused on him.

His mind tried to piece the information together – a gestalt, the monkey from his psychology lessons working out how to leave the cage with just a stick and a banana (*Kohler, that's it, Kohler, Gestalt, how the whole is greater than the sum of its parts, insight learning*), Eureka moments *(he's going to smack my brother),* all of it coming together *(he's coming),* we do not learn through reward and punishment, but through Holistic insights, *(on his way, geez, he's a tall lad),* and he could see Polo veer slightly away from the mob, arching his head slightly, bowing, pace increasing *(he's going to hit my brother),* the others beginning to grin, fists clenching, a foot away, a foot away *(my little brother),* and suddenly, *suddenly,* the caged chimpanzee in that experiment *(little county)* whose name, if HobNob remembered correctly, was Roland, unlocks the

145

door miraculously, to the applause of the German experimenters and everything goes still... completely still...

HobNob watches Polo, slow motion.

One step forward.

(He's going to punch my brother)

(His violent eyes)

(Unlike you cunts)

Bull, aware, standing, ready,

(my little brother)

The chimpanzee...

(hit him)

...stands on two legs and bows...

(hit him)

...to the audience of...

(my little brother)

...thrilled German experimenters with...

(HIT THE CUNT)

...spectacular bow ties...

Whooooooooooooooooooosh...kerrrrrack!!!

HobNob's lightning right hook accompanied by an echo, like the sound of a cracking whip, connected with the assailants nose just before he hit his younger brother.

A tremendous punch.

Fast, forceful, infused with suppressed venom and unconscious velocity and perfectly targeted.

Polo fell to the floor awkwardly; his head cracking on the concrete, bouncing like a 5kg medicine ball.

Clever, HobNob, Bull said. Top punch.

Roland, HobNob replied, nonsensically, looking at the remaining eleven Peterborough lads who it appeared, were stunned.

They had no idea what to do next.

An echoing silence.

(*Gunfight at the OK Corral.*)

(*The Wild Bunch.*)

(*Tumbleweed...the wind whistles...*)

Taxis on the rank outside waited for passengers who were taking their time.

Students with rucsacs stopped reading their music papers.

A married couple – the woman wearing an inexpensive, flowerless pink hat as if she had just attended the wedding celebrations of a distant cousin she didn't know very well and probably didn't like very much – tried to hurry past, but found themselves simultaneously transfixed and horrified.

A man with Lennon specs looked up from his Notes on Wittgenstein paperback.

A passing conductor reached for his radio.

Man down, shocked, bleeding.

Eleven men.

Statuesque, the moment pregnant with uncertainty and anticipation.

Peterborough.

Two men.
The moment full of fear and endings.
Notts.

Distant time.
Dead time.
Frozen time.

Whispers from the witnesses…

And…
…then…
…they turn to look at each other…

Fuck it, Bull says, looking at his brother. Vikings? Vikings, HobNob replied.

And as one, they began to scream.
AAAAAAAAAAAAAAAAAAAAAAAAAAAAAAA
AAAAAAAAAAAAAAAAAAAAAAAAAAAAAAA
AAAAAAAAAAAAAAAAAAAAAAAAAAAAAAA
AAAAAAAAAAAAAAAAAAAAAAAAAAAAAAA
AAAAAAAAAAAAAAAAAAAAAAAAAAAAAAA

AAAAAAAAAAAAAAAAAAAAAAAAAAAAAAAAAAA
AAAAAAAAAAAAAAAAAAAAAAAAAAAAAAAAAAA
AAAAAAAAAAAAAAAAAAAAAAAAAAAAAAAAAAA
AAAAAAAAAAAAAAAAAAAAAAAAAAAAAAAAAAA
AAAAAAAAAAAAAAAAAAAAAAAAAAAAAAAAAAA
AAAAAAAAAAAAAAAAAAAAAAAAAAAAAAAAAAA
AAAAAAAAAAAAAAAAAAAAAAAAAAAAAAAAAAA
AAAAAAAAAAAAAAAAAAAAAAAAAAAAAAAAAAA
AAAAAAAAAAAAAAAAAAAARRRRRRRRRRRRRRR
RRRRRRRRRRRRRRRRRRRRRRRRRRRRRRRRRRR
RRRRRRRRRRRRRRRRRRRRRRRRRRRRRRRRRRR
RRRRRRRRRRRRRRRRRRRRRRRRRRRRRRRRRRR
RRRRRRRRRRRRRRRRRRRRRRRRRRRRRRRRRRR
RRRRRRRRRRRRRRRRRRRRRRRRRRRRRRRRRRR
RRRRRRRRRRRRRRRRRRRRRRRRRRRRRRRRRRR
RRRRGGGGGGGGGGGGGGGGGGGGGGGGGGGGGGG
GGGGGGGGGGGGGGGGGGGGGGGGGGGGGGGGGGG
GGGGGGGGGGGGGGGGGGGGGGGGGGGGGGGGGGG
GGGGGGGGGGGGGGGGGGGGGGGGGGGGGGGGGGG
GGGGGGGGGGGGGGGGGGGGGGGGGGGGGGGGGGG
GGGGGGGGGGGGGGGGGGGGGGGGGGGGGGGGGGG
GGGGGGGGGGGGGGGGGGGGGGGGGGGGGGGGGGG
GGGGGGGGGGGGGGGGGGGGGGGGGGGGGGGGGGG
GGGGGGGGGGGGGGGGGGGGGGGGGGGGGGGGGGG
GGGGGGGGGGGGGGGGGGGGGHHHHHHHHHHH
HHHHHHHHHHHHHHHHHHIIIIIIIIIHHHHHHHHHHH
HHHHHHHHHHHHHHHHHHHHHHHHHHHHHHHHHHH
HHHHHHHHHHHHHHHHHHHHHHHHHHHHHHHHHHH
HHHHHHHHHHHHHHHHHHHHHHHHHHHHHHHHHHH
HHHHHHHHHHHHHHHHHHHHHHHHHHHHHHHHHHH
HHHHHHHHHHHHHHHHHHHHHHHHHHHHHHHHHHH
AAAAAAAAAAAAAAAAAAAAAAAAAAAAAAAAAAA
AAAAAAAAAAAAAAAAAAAAAAAAAAAAAAAAAAA
AAAAAAAAAAAAAAAAAAAAAAAAAAAAAAAAAAA
AAAAAAAAAAAAAAAAAAAAAAAAAAAAAAAAAAA
AAAAAAAAAAAAAAAAAAAAAAAAARRRRRRRRR
RRRRRRRRRRRRRRRRRRRRRRRRRRRRRRRRRRR
RRRRRRRRRRRRRRRRRRRRRRRRRRRRRRRRRRR
RRRRRRRRRRRRRRRRRRRRRRRRRRRRRRRRRRR
RRRRRRRRRRRRRRRRRRRRGGGGGGGGGGGGGGG

GGGGGGGGGGGGGGGGGGGGGGGGGGGGGGGGGGG
GGGGGGGGGGGGGGGGGGGGGGGGGGGGGGGGGGG
GGGGGGGGGGGGGGGGGGGGGGGGGGGGGGGGGGG
GHHHHHHHHHHHHHHHHHHHHHHHHHHHHHHHH
HHHHHHHHHHHHHHHHHHHHHHHHHHHHHHHHH
HHHHHHHHHHHHHHHHHHHHHHHHH…

…Bull floored one, a bleached cheeked old boy with a goatee, getting even, fraternal rivalry. HobNob nutted another, the impact landed with a sickening bang, fracturing the bridge of his nose, specks of exploding adenoidal blood flying around his diddyman haircut like crimson silkworms. Bull split the lip of one and kicked another, the victim falling to the floor. Another butted, his head bouncing off the concrete like Polo earlier. Another slap, a series of slaps, one, two, three lads, crisp and clear connections, a whirlwind, a Catherine wheel, premium speed fireworks, guaranteed explosions, superspeed, nothing to lose: A daisycutter, one of those bombs that explodes just a foot off the ground, a helicopter action, a windmill whirling, another, another…

…the Peterborough, surprised, stunned; no idea how to respond, flight or fight (or do nothing), and all the way through, slap after butt after boot, the Bully brothers did not stop screaming, did not stop screeching, their indignant, suicidal berserker rage (Norsemen landing on the coast of Lindisfarne, the Danes at Stamford Bridge, the Normans at Hastings on their chargers), they never, ever stopped their insane cries…

…AAAAAAAAAAAAAAAAAAAAAAAAAAAAAAA
AAAAAAAAAAAAAAAAAAAAAAAAAAAAAAAAA
AAAAAAAAAAAAAAAAAAAAAAAAAAAAAAAAA
AAAAARRRRRRRRRRRRRRRRRRRRRRRRRRRR
RRRRRRRRRRRRRRRRRRRRRRRRRRRRRRRRRR
RRRGGGGGGGGGGGGGGGGGGGGGGGGGGGGGG
GGGGGGGGGGGGGGGGGGGGGGGGGGGGGGGGG
GGGGGGGGGGGGGHHHHHHHHHHHHHHHHHHH
HHHHHHHHHHHHHHHHHHHHHHHHHHHHHHHHH
HHHHHHHHHHHHHHHHHHHHHHHHHHHHHHHHH
HHHH…and the impact of those screams shattered

Peterborough. Broke their resolve, the sheer ferocity of it, the total *chutzpah* of it, and the bloody *cheek* of it.

Two stick twelve.

Two stick.

Now six stick two.

Five of them on their toes, heading toward the platform, scuttling down the stairs as fast as their legs could carry them with Bull chasing, punching, whacking, smacking, cracking, nutting, lamping, bashing, slapping, battering, kicking, booting, screaming, crying, yelping, shrieking.

HobNob fighting with two braver hybrids, whacking one, taking two good ones back, a cygnet ring connected with his top teeth, a boot in his belly, a crack on his ear. Fights back with a deafening headbutt, the impact of which sounded like a depth charge exploding against the side of a ship made of bone. The buttbag, frizzy haired, grey combat jacket, fell to the ground, bleeding, and he got up, shook his head, gave it all up as a bad job and scarpered toward the platform. Another faced with the screaming, and the madness ran back out onto the road, further away from the last train.

One stood; HobNob punched him in the mouth. He hit back, a good one, which floored the Notts man, the floor a dangerous place to be, but the Posh allowed him to get back up. They're fighting like boxers. Butting, clouting, thumping, screaming, WAR, WAR, WAR, WAR, WAR, WAR, and Bull returned from his runabout and helped his brother, landing a blinding volley, which connected squarely on his ear and the hybrid fell. Not wasting a second, Bull fly kicked a newly refreshed Polo, returned him to the cold comfort of the floor, dragged another, slapped him six or seven times on the nose, left him dazed on the precipice of the platform's top step…

…and HobNob, noticing out of the corner of his eye on the other side of the concourse the automatic doors opening, admitting more Peterborough, gestured to Bull, who winked cheekily at the stricken young lad on the station concourse decking, and trotted off toward the exit.

Amazingly, Ginger from the Fellows appeared.

The strident Ginger.
The orator.
The Herald of the Peterborough Legions of Darkness.
The Scourge of the Land.

The Hardest Team in the Fourth Tier.
Mighty Peterborough.
Mighty Ginger.

Bull tapped him on the shoulder – *your lads are scrapping with ours down there, it's a fucking bloodbath* – and Ginger, baffled, uncomprehending, gestured to his mates and they ran toward the top of the staircase chasing phantom Notts.

The Bully brothers turned round to watch them, only to see an enraged Polo and another beefy Posh lad run toward them. They looked at each other, decided enough was enough, and ran down toward Broad Marsh, past the Bentinck, past the Tote, past the bus stops, past the bridge over the canal, past the cycle shop and the Carrington chippy, occasionally turning round to see an athletic (and bloody) Polo chasing them, and laughing all the way down, the brothers, two stick, *(little county...)* two stick TWELVE (*county's got no lads*), laughing until they found themselves in (*unlike you cunts*) Broad Marsh bogs, in a cubicle, tears rolling down their faces, breathless...

8. Last Match of the Season

Coventry City used to be a Star Soccer staple, with Hugh Johns and Co only occasionally venturing further east than Leicester, and that was usually to visit Forest.

Stoke, Wolves, the Baggies, Birmingham (with the magnificent, moustachioed Bob Hatton), Villa (with the wonderful refrain of *Shit on the Villa, Shit on the Villa Today*), and Coventry, who held some sort of record for staying in the old first division.

Coventry had fared even worse than Notts, a modern fall from grace story involving all the usual suspects: Incompetent managers, bad appointments, which even the most idiotic of supporters knew were bound to fail; inadequate governance, straw man directors, corrupt, vainglorious, overambitious small town millionaires spraying the ether with big ideas and fat cigars.

Terrible overpaid players, plain old bad luck – the type that never ends. A titanic albatross of a stadium, a reverberating white elephant modelled on NFL lines that the club could neither fill nor afford, and finally, to cap it all off, brutal knife-in-the-back betrayal when the fans least expected it. Mark Robins heading north to Huddersfield after taking the Sky Blues to within an inch of the league one playoffs.

Worse, for them, the town of Coventry had just begun to buzz.

Nothing worse than that, despair plucked from the jaws of victory, learned helplessness denied and confirmed. They hate him now, do the Sky Blues. They hate him more than some of the other crazed limpets who tried and failed to save an old Star Soccer staple, and in their enthusiasm and self-belief, only left them deeper in the mire.

I described this to HobNob, Mini-Beefy and Bull in the Fellows, but at least two of them weren't listening, having spotted a mob of twenty five burly Coventry walking towards the Lloyds on the Canal.

Still a first division firm, HobNob said

More of the Should Know Better Club, Bull replied.

Like us. We got history with them?

I think Staffy and his gang got involved outside Broad Marsh in the old first division. Eighty one, eighty two.

I don't remember that, Bull said. Who won?

Just a runabout in-between the buses. One Tuesday night. I think the result was inconclusive. I also heard that there was a meet at Watford Gap. Coppers got involved, sharpish, and that was the end of that. I've not heard fuck all happening away. They're one of those teams who exist on another planet to us.

Who do they hate? Mini-Beefy asked.

Leicester and Villa, his dad replied. Huge rivalry with Leicester.

Leicester hate every fucker, Bull said.

Baby Squad.

Still crazy after all these years. I mean, Baby Squad. Over-forties should know better club. They need a new name.

It's a brand, HobNob. Can't change a brand with forty years of history.

What, like Snickers? I call them Marathons. Yet another example of incipient and overarching American cultural imperialism.

What, changing the name of the Baby Squad?

No, Snickers. Do you remember that time they came down for that Full Members Cup match?

I do, Bull said, grinning. Six thousand of them for a night match at the old ground.

The Baby Squad...

...thirty of them arrived in the Roadside, Baby Squad, hundreds of us in the old wooden shack underneath the condemned stand, a relic of the early twentieth, and they stood down the front as bold as brass, and we ran down the front, forty or fifty of us. They never moved, and we stopped, knowing that if we continued the momentum from the wooden stand onto the terracing below, into the maw of the Baby Squad, we would probably be cut to pieces.

The situation reminded me of being on one of those old siege engines in the Crusades.

Level with the ramparts of the castle, the exit plank goes down – so which daft cunt is going to be the first across when the doors open with the boiling oil, and the flaming arrows pointed your way?

Same that night. No one wanted to go first.

The Squaddies were in there for one reason, and they stood. Mixture of shadeys, casuals, skinheads and normals. Denim jackets and jeans. Baseball caps and tracksuit tops. Boots and trainers. Ages ranging from twenty five to fifty – and this was in nineteen ninety! The civilians scattered, all the family fans, and there was a space between them and us in the stands down there on the fence. I remember making eye contact with one of them, a wiry geezer in a white and blue Ellesse tennis tracksuit top. He gestured to the side of the stand for me and him to go down those wooden stairs to sort it out, and I knew that if I had gone, I would not be here to tell you this story, or if I had been, I would have been talking to you with a third smile running vertically down my chubby cheeks.

I didn't shit it – well, I did a bit – but they were a top ten firm and they don't shake hands afterwards. Had the Baby Squad been in the trenches in France on Christmas Day 1914, they wouldn't be playing football in no man's land with the Boche. You only had to look at them. I personally think that pound-for-pound, they were the hardest firm I ever saw down the old ground. Professionals. This is what they did. This is how they got their kicks. We had the numbers that day, but they had the track record, the brand and the reputation.

And the blades, the decorator's knives, the Stanleys, the Kitchen Devils.

What happened?

They took our end, waited for the filth to arrive, grinned and jumped over the side onto the cinder track over to the Kop.

Bastards!

... and I've never forgotten that.

I know, I was standing next to you. I don't think you would have enjoyed it if you'd have gone round the back.

No. I wouldn't. You're right, he replied.

There was silence for a moment. Bull picked up his pint of Witches Nipple, downed a half pint in one, turned to his brother ostentatiously and said.

You still shat it, HobNob.

We all laughed.

I know. Not one of my finest moments, HobNob said. Who wants more ale?

Witches for me, Bull replied

Same, I said, taking a good guzzle of the wheaty, yeasty dregs and then sliding over the pint glass.

Mini-Beefy sat and sipped at his coke. He was saying nothing as usual. I often wonder what he actually thought of his dad and uncle, their antics, their seriously immature (and risky) behaviour. In the end, I got the impression that he thought his dad and uncle should grow up a bit, but he never said anything.

What time are we meeting the rest?

They're coming out of Lloyds in ten, Bull said. Let's get these down our necks and join them.

The Procession! It has to be done!

Yes, the Procession. The Homage. We'll go down the TBI for a few more. I'm getting the taste for this.

HobNob nodded. Yep.

I finished my beer before the rest of them and stood up, stretched my legs.

Bull wore a royal blue bomber jacket with the ostentatious zip, like a hoop earring, all the way to the top. Blue jeans and brown boots. HobNob wore specs, a black shirt, blue jeans and Chelsea boots. The only person wearing a brand was Mini-Beefy, his kagoule-like sports blouson imprinted with a V. As usual, I looked like the geek I am, but substantially thinner than the two brothers.

We all departed by the conservatory entrance.

Over the other side of the canal, we could see the Notts gather.

I wonder whether they've seen those Cov, HobNob said as we walked up the cobbles to the Boulevard.

Far too early for a setpiece. If it goes off at all, it'll go off after. Coventry will be having a pint next door, he said, pointing to the Via Fossa. I mean look...

Adjacent to the courthouse, a wagonload of yellow-jacketed police watched the situation develop on canalside. Twenty years ago, it would already have gone off down here, Coventry on one side, Notts on the other.

A blaze of colour, a flurry of fists and boots. A berserker cry (c'mon then, c'mon then), back and forward, back and forward, twenty-on-twenty, fists connecting with shallow sockets, thumbs in eyes, teeth parting from gums, yelps, cries, boots upside your head, trainers stamping, conscious, unconscious, running about, always running about.

Not today.

Not down here, in 2013, the regenerated canalside, full of upmarket brasseries selling champagne at a hundred quid a bottle. Chain wine bars, chain eateries, chain charcuteries, chain hairdressers where grown men spend thirty seven pounds on a Danny Craig haircut; student chain comedy clubs full of tedious student comics taking the piss out of people in wheelchairs and making prehistoric observations about the battle of the sexes.

One hundred and thirty five quid a month gyms with mixed saunas.

Running through the opulence is the reanimated canal, recently biologically dead; stinking of death and shit and the lethal chemicals that fuelled the British industrial revolution, won us the Second World War and left behind a toxic disaster area replete with piles of unguent, softened, semi-dissolved hybrid fish. A waterway bursting with the vile leftovers of the narcissistic sixties generation, our parents and grandparents, who took all the money for their houses and pensions, and thus, looted our futures, swapped our future well being for idleness and a non-stop retirement holiday abroad. Now scrubbed, scoured, eviscerated, defenestrated, strained and drained, pristine blue, full of fish.

The occasional brightly painted barge passing by.

Historical fictionists, retired local authority housing officers, community development workers, chartered accountants, social workers and early years co-ordinators living the dream and embracing the freedom.

Windswept gulls and hunting falcons waiting to feast on newly spawned carp, tench, pike and bream. Hen parties chock full of pre-loaded married women looking for young bucks to fuck in the rat runs behind the Oceana. Pre-loaded stag nights full of coked-up bravos from Derby, and Hednesford, and Rochdale, and Stamford. Lincoln, and Beverley, and Brighton, and Rainham.

Two young women walked hand-in-hand along the canal wearing printed flowery dresses and gold thong sandals. They looked very much in love, but they could be just friends. In front of the new magistrates court, rode a cyclist wearing an ill-fitting rose-pink helmet on a mountain bike costing four thousand seven hundred quid. Young, self-assured, self-aware, politically neutral, transmetropolitan, fit, with communication skills honed at a redbrick university, empathetic, health conscious, green, gender sensitive, racially relaxed and already a three star cook in his own fitted kitchen (with metallic oven and granite worktops), he was heading toward Trent Bridge on the tow path running all the way past the heat station and the old caves.

Past Meadow Lane.

The canal is his.

The world is his.

People everywhere.

Young and old passing through a kaleidoscope of modern colour. Below us, a character in a charcoal fleece and expensive frameless glasses sat on a pub bench on the canalside, watching the world go by. An impossibly handsome Airedale by his side, newly trimmed and groomed, ears pricked, awaiting the fulsome attention of passers-by. An unopened Graham Greene novel beside him, lying flat, next to a pint of some obscure amber ale whose translucent head, the colour of pistachio shells, and swirling just-poured fog is the liquid equivalent of an idea whose time has come at last.

Who would want to spend such a splendid weekend at such a splendid place cooped up at Central Station, staring at the face of Jesus on the wall of a stinking cell the size of a toilet?

Shaking hands and nodding as appropriate, the Bullys, Mini-Beefy and I joined the Procession about to happen. Crumble and his gang – the last men to actually brawl outside the old Bentinck (in the station, in the Tesco Express), three years ago – were at the front. Bull wandered over to say hello, the old generation and the middle generation meeting; and the young lads on their mobiles, many of who wouldn't remember the Bentinck in its jaded, skittish, raffish pomp, there to show respect.

Staffy was there with his mob. Old school. Johnny T and his three lads. The Bestwood mob. About fifty, mostly in modern sportswear, the uniform of the post-millennial casual – blues and browns and greys.

Camouflage, not as obvious on the CCTV cameras.

Crumble signalled to the rest.

They began to walk up toward the Station along the canal.

Mini-Beefy tapped his dad on the shoulder.

Look there, dad, he said, pointing to where we had come from.

Over on the other side of the canal, next to the pub we had just been drinking in, was the Via Fossa. On its top balcony, standing and watching the situation were the Coventry gang seen earlier. Older, more homogenous than the Notts. Winter colours, almost black jackets. All of them over forty. Most of them with Russian skinheads. Clean-shaven.

Holding pint glasses like weapons, unsmiling predators.
Watching.
That's their main boys, Beef, HobNob said.
Will there be trouble later?
I reckon, son.
You're not getting involved are you, dad?

No, son. Past it.

I know. You're fifty next year.

Fifty?

What was granddad doing when he was fifty? Beefy asked as they walked off Canalside.

Working, son. He always worked on Saturdays. Wouldn't be doing this, HobNob replied.

By the way, dad. What *are* we going to do?

When we get to the Bentinck, stay on this side of the road. If it gets tasty, I'll meet you down there at the fireplace warehouse, and we'll walk down to the Lane through the Meadows.

But, dad...

Don't worry, son. There's going to be no trouble. This is purely political. Just glad that there are others about with the same sense of tradition.

But it was just a dirty pub that nobody used, dad, Mini-Beefy said, a serious mien, which told his dad that he meant what he said, that there was no doubt or internal prevarication, no subconscious debate.

The Bentinck to him was exactly that.

A dirty pub.

Not to me, Beef. Not to me, his dad said.

And he meant it.

Bull approached me as we stood outside the Bentinck, which had recently become a Guatemala Joe's, egregious, ubiquitous style symbol, according to HobNob, of the climax of incipient American Cultural Imperialism and the Transmetropolitan Takeover.

The outside had been whitewashed with emulsion and the forest green corporate iconography was prominent in big letters underneath the upstairs windows. Windows, which by all accounts, were fronts for hotel rooms, only not run by Guatemala Joe's.

I wondered how a customer would access them and how much. I felt like renting a room just to get the complete picture. *How did one rent a room? Who owned the rooms? Who profited? Were they clean?* The Bullys' tales of the Bentinck led me to believe the Hotel would have been a pit, a vermin-infested hovel that should have been demolished for public safety, but would it have been perceived as such a fleapit in the eighties before the immaculately clean – and shockingly bland – Dick Whittington Inn takeover, where each room is the same from Brighton to Aberdeen, and your stay would be a mollified experience of magnolia wallpaper, commercial shower gel, lockable coat hangers, chessboard-mirror tiles, twenty TV channels and nowhere near enough pillows and blankets. By contrast, you can imagine the Bentinck Hotel room. The stink of air freshener hiding the cigar trails and the nutty beer stains. Sheets left unchanged on the bed. Certainly two or three guests worth. A used condom lurking underneath the counterpane. Velvet curtains too expensive to dry clean. Cigarette butts abandoned in un-emptied ashtrays: Carpet – an insect rainforest nirvana. A dial-telephone connected straight to the bar. Room service. A sausage sandwich and a pint of lager. The midnight horror film: *The Beast Must Die. The Reptile. Blood on Satan's Claw. The Gorgon. Witchfinder General. Race with the Devil.* More blankets than you can handle, be it winter or summer. A peasants' fruit bowl next to the television, an apple, an orange and a banana, all plastic, even down to the apple sprig. A blotter, a writing pad and an imitation fountain pen with no cartridge. George, mopping up a pint jug with a filthy towel in his military blue shirt, immaculate striped tie and brilliantined hair, shoes, which shone like the absorbent patina of a black hole in space, pulling every centimetre of light from around them, giving you a wink when you take the fragrant Sneinton tart you met in the Exchange – black-seamed stockings, red high-heel shoes, lacy panties and thick, crimson lipstick – up the back stairs, straight to the back passage.

I could see why the boys were angry.

Guatemala Joe's, like the Dick Whittington Inn, was the opposite of everything.

An anti-culture, an anti-message, a negative zone, an asinine, one-dimensional, con trick designed for a sole purpose – to make Mr Guatemala Joe richer than Croesus and fuck the socio-cultural costs. Fuck the impact on the psychosphere.

Looking around the Guatemala Joe's – and the people in it from all over the world, all young, all intelligent, all staring at iPhone screens, each of which cost more than George's weekly wage, all of them drinking coffee, each variety of which cost more than any pint ever sold on George's watch.

All these young people, the bright-eyed and bushy-tailed staff in pretty black blouses, even the men, the transmetropolitan men, now looking at the football hooligans standing around the windows outside, staring inward, faces touched by the void, like the zombies waiting to attack the mall in *Dawn of the Dead.*

Everyone stopped what they were doing.

Staff.

Coffeeists.

Bull.

Me.

I sat on a spare stool. A boy next to me, no more than eighteen, pipe-cleaner thin, wearing a smart cardigan and strides, with a Danny Craig RAF style haircut, parting carefully gelled, almost sculpted, leaving a gavelled, distinct trench that must have taken an hour to create in front of the mirror, stopped typing into his laptop. A young man named Levis, in a beige kagoule, stared at him through the window, a look, which slowly turned from benign and blank, an undead look, into a look of pure hatred.

At the window next to me, Staffy and a punk I didn't recognise stared at two Chinese students as if they were responsible for a death in the family.

The realisation hit me.

They're going to batter every diner in the Guatemala Joe's, I thought.

I have to get out of here.

This was taking my mission to its extreme.

I wanted to write a book, not be party to a violent assault.

I felt my heart race and a dark feeling descend upon me.

In that moment, I hated Bull and HobNob for involving me in this, hated them, hated…

Bull appeared next to me, a moment of psychic connection.

It's not what you think. Watch this.

Crumble walked up to the counter.

I'll ey an Americano and two Muffins, me duck.

The Scandinavian-looking woman behind the counter didn't do any sales talk or offer her name, or do any of the other Guatemala Joe's stuff she was trained to do with civilians.

She just nodded.

Young Jake went to the counter.

He did the same. Latte and two muffins, duck, he said.

Breaker next. Nick. Beech. A couple of lads I didn't know.

All of them.

All the lads from outside began to queue up.

I noticed Levis blow young Danny Craig a kiss as he came in. HobNob joined the queue as did Mini-Beefy, which I didn't expect. He must have convinced his son of the rightness of his cause. Little Dave and Big Eddie, a mate from HobNob's days in the flats, always well turned out. Clarkson and Philpot. The three Pauls. Breaker, who had appeared from nowhere. Whisky Jack and some of his Newark bloods, big fans of the Bentinck.

One-by-one, they ordered a coffee and two cakes.

Universal.

Messy creamy cakes.

Milky coffees.

One coffee. Two cakes.

They paid their money and took their coffee and cakes, cleaning out the refreshments frontage, nothing left, leaving a panicked manager with his finger on the button of a mobile phone programmed straight for the coppers.

The Notts lads chatted amiably, but they didn't touch their coffee and their cakes until the last man, which happened to be Bestwood Paul, in his green polo shirt and Hackett cap.

Crumble looked outside the door.

Gestured to someone.

Stood in the centre of the now-packed Guatemala Joe's, halfway between the counter and the door.

The Notts stopped talking.

Everyone else stopped doing the things they usually do in the coffee shop.

The laptops, the iPhones, the Kindles. They stopped sipping their coffees.

A tense hush. Tranquillity.

It seemed to me to last hours. If, as Graham Greene said, that eternity is an absolute absence of time, as I sat there, it felt as if time had frozen and judging by the faces of those around me, I guessed I wasn't the only one.

All was still.

Crumble made himself big and tall like they tell you to do in the manuals when you need to demonstrate authority, and began to shout a prearranged signal.

GIVE US OUR PUB BACK! He shouted and poured his coffee in an arc along the floor and the frontage full of cakes, making sure it dripped slowly on the newly laid laminated planks in spatters and gobbets. Taking aim with real purpose, he then threw a lemon curd muffin at the blackboard behind the counter.

Together, as one, they all did the same. All the muffin grenades and cream cake missiles flew like a Stalin's Organ fusillade toward the counter, showering the cowering staff in cream, sultanas and pastry, the counter quickly turning into a thick sugary mess. The perfectly polished and varnished floor was soon awash with coffee, and the hapless diners (and their manbags, laptops, iPhones, male grooming products and thirty seven quid haircuts), left as fast as they could by any entrance they could find.

I could see Bull laughing from the depth of his chest.

Six or seven of the younger lads, scarves wrapped around their faces, quickly and skilfully branded the tables with NCFC signs in black and white on each window-mounted table, the blowback from the paint tins spraying the windows. Photos were taken. The manager would have called the police, but he was covered in blueberry muffin detritus and his mobile phone had been knocked into the sink.

Someone kicked in the dessert frontage with heavy boots and the tubular, glass-fronted structure, polished to a sunburst shine, shattered into a thousand pieces. A quick look at Crumble told me he wasn't happy with that, it was one over the top, but I didn't care, because by this time, I was running down toward London Road, past the Tesco Express, the old Zaks nightclub, the old Granby, the Homeless Arts Centre and the Jobcentre, toward Boots and the old Hooters hahahahahahahahahhahahhahahahahahahah ....we had all split up, some running past The Medz towards the Meadows, some heading toward the Vat and Fiddle with the beardy weirdies discussing structural differences in hop fermentation between Bishop's Mitre and The Scold's Bridle microbrews (from Carlisle and Northampton, respectively), and some ran back into town.

HobNob and Mini-Beefy ran with me, laughing all the way, Bull quietly merging into the crowd and going back into Broad Marsh, taxicab plans, knowing that we would meet him later. The wind buffeted my escape, and I'm not that fit, so it was hard and when we reached the wall outside Hooters, where we sat, six of us, rolling, I could scarcely breathe.

While they talked, I took a step away from the rest of them and stared at the sky, analysing what we had just done.

I'm a thirty something professional writer.

I write manuals, bids, articles and novels. I am the writer of the decent selling Notts County hooligan novel *Ultra Violence*. I have A Levels and a degree in English Literature. I have travelled to thirty-one countries. I have money in the bank, and a future ahead of me, and here I was running away from a Guatemala Joe's, wrecked in an act of corporate terrorism.

Petty revenge for a dirty old pub.

Their dirty old pub. *Our* dirty old pub.

If the coppers caught me, I would be busted and my reputation possibly ruined.

Bull would lose his job for sure.

A decent job.

As could the others.

It was a strange world now. I had seen this in the past two years, mixing with these Nottingham men, these men at least a decade older than me, who looked at the world in a different way. I had seen the world through their eyes, and they didn't like it. They didn't feel they belonged, this new world.

It had become an alien planet.

A world of conformity.

A world of obsessive cleanliness and order.

A world where the trains ran on time.

A world where authority is respected rather than challenged.

A world of police.

A world of voids.

A world that worships money and nice things.

A world for women.

A world shaped by women for women.

A world of shallow romance, of celebrity, of sex, of fashion and of the pre-eminence of good looks, the triumph of the surface over meaning.

A world where female managers have made drinking at dinner a taboo and joking in the workplace unacceptable.

A world where the welfare state is a tired anachronism.

A world of seriousness.

A sententious world.

A capricious world.

A world of self-absorption.

A world where internet fuelled narcissism is venerated and encouraged.

A world of Photo-Me websites and social networks.

A world where your neighbour is a stranger and the local pub is dead.

A world without anarchy.

A world the Bully brothers and their friends did not recognise.

An American world.

A world where those in the demonstration today did not belong.
A world, which had left them behind.
A world represented by Guatemala Joe's.

I felt my heart beat, and I could understand why the other five of them – HobNob, his son Mini-Beefy, Levis, Staffy and Breaker – were chortling like hyenas as if they had just been told the funniest joke in the world by someone hilariously funny.

After that, the game was always going to be an anti-climax.

9. Tommy's Bar

At half time, HobNob sat next to Renfield in Tommy's Bar, and I went over and joined them, wanting to meet him, a proper name at Meadow Lane, and someone I'd not met before.

He sat there, smart in his modish Lacoste, jeans and boots, clean-shaven and clippered (but not skinheaded). He looked at me warily, but HobNob introduced us.

It turned out he had read *Ultra Violence* and enjoyed it. Renfield had been military once, in his younger days, British Army, Foreign Legion some said, and he had seen active service, but nowadays he did something in import-export.

Not many people inquired any further than that, so I wasn't going to.

We talked for a bit.

Renfield complained that I hadn't made the Notts gang hard enough in *Ultra Violence* and that I was overly eager to stress how minor they all were.

I mean, he said, a bit drunk and earnest, Forest are down to a hundred now, if that. Probably less. You think we're old cunts? They're all even older. They're past it. All dead or claiming pensions. They don't bother going. Notts have more lads – more young lads any road. Anyway, forget them – if you want a scrap, you have to go lower division. Conference...Alfreton Town versus Grimsby. Grimsby versus Mansfield. Any contest involving Lincoln. Look at Nuneaton. 80 arrests. 150 old LTE trapped on a Nuneaton Council Estate. Three hundred locals putting the windows through. A thousand coppers keeping them apart. Planned for months. Look at Stockport vs Kiddy last week. Rioting in the Town Centre. There's no trouble in the EPL. You'd be lucky to find a Chelsea hooligan nowadays. Fuck the *Football Factory*...I mean, you may as well read historical fiction as that cunt. Nah, Forest has been over-policed for years and the young uns come down here. No coppers.

Don't they get on now? HobNob asked. Notts and Forest?

Renfield wiped his nose on the back of his hand and nodded. Yep. Not like our day.

Times change.

They certainly do, Hobbers.

In front of us, Clifton Tom was drinking another pint of bitter. Crumble and Scally were pogoing. Paul was arguing with someone about the merits of living in Basford. Arnold Paul was telling me something I didn't understand because he was pissed, and I was busy being dazzled by his emerald green kagoule.

Someone, somewhere, started singing...

Oh, Notts County...the only football team to come from Nottingham...

...and Renfield joined in loudly and ostentatiously. Bull came over and shook hands with him, mates from long past. He brought eight shiny cans of Red Stripe with him and passed two each to us all. Mini-Beefy sneakily nipped at one of HobNob's cans, and I knew he was going to a party that evening, and who was I to get moral about it all? I was starting to feel a bit woozy, the endless drink going down. It was not even half past three. On the pitch behind the bar, the rather sterile game being played in front of seven thousand increasingly chilly and uninterested people, continued to its inevitable first half conclusion. I calculated that I had drunk eight pints to this point. In my student days, eight pints would have seen me on the sofa asleep, and I would suffer a dreadful hangover the next day. Today, I was going strong, a mixture of experience, excitement and the desire not to stop. HobNob and Bull drank two drinks to my one and neither showed any ill effects. I guess it didn't hurt that they didn't touch the large quantities of drugs the rest of them were sampling in the toilets – the crack, the coke, the speed, which amplified the impact of each pint by a vector of five.

Scally was speeding, singing a song about Lee Hughes coming back next year with Port Vale, and how he would happily give him a wank. He sang this song without embarrassment and as he did so, he made hand gestures rather like the pistons of a steam train. The lad works for the government in some capacity and I grinned when I remembered this.

The departure of Hughes at Keith Curle's behest was the turning point of the season and feelings ran high in Tommy's Bar.

Renfield rose and joined in another chant with Chas the Mod who was utterly out of it, his right eye going one way and his left going another as he danced to some music that only he could hear. He is a legendary drinker with an enormous capacity. He stopped and told Bull that he had tickets for the Stone Roses reunion gig on Wigan Pier and everyone who heard him say this believed it, and was officially envious, including me. He asked HobNob for a racing tip, but the older Bully brother ignored him with a grin, and I realised it was a private joke between them. Mini-Beefy came over as more and more people came in Tommy's Bar to escape the wind and watch the scores on Sky Sports. (Doncaster Brentford 0-0. Barnet in big trouble and Wimbledon safe.)

HobNob leaned over and spoke to me while Bull and the import-exporter were deep in conversation.

Renfield told me a great story.

What? I replied.

When Notts were shit and after Bull and I were warned off by the filth, quite a few Notts went elsewhere for their jollies. Many – including Jools, Breaker, the Calverton mob, Percy and that – all went to follow England. Some – who shall remain nameless – even followed Forest for a bit, because you were guaranteed a good battle if you ran with that lot at the time, though as you heard Renfield say, perhaps not recently. Some of them went further afield, and Renfield ran with Stoke for a couple of seasons. He scrapped all over the shop – St Andrews, that major pitched battle with Preston on the M6, Subway Army – and he worked his way up through the ranks until he started running with the N40, the real ringleaders. They got their name in the early eighties after forty of them went on a train to Pompey and caused havoc – small scale violence as opposed to their usual brand of mass disorder. Remember what I told you about the time they tried to overturn a train full of Carlisle at Derby station? That's not hooliganism – that's political! They're a force of nature, them cunts. Anyway, he gets his slippers well tucked under the table, and he was invited to Birmingham for a morning constitutional in Balsall Heath with the Zulus. Two van loads. Forty hand-picked men. Not kids. Not casuals. Proper fighting. Proper man's stuff. He was happy with that, considered it an honour and met up one Saturday morning in Burton. They picked him up and soon they were sitting in the back of a van behind a wasteground in Balsall Heath. He's sitting there and he doesn't mind admitting he was shitting himself. There's a toolbox in the back of the van and some meaty geezer opened it and started distributing the goods. Renfield found himself holding a five pound lump hammer, and he stuck it in his pocket. Some bloke, who looked like an accountant, slid a machete into his tracksuit top. Another, a cleaver. Stanleys, flare guns, claw hammers, Yankee screwdrivers, extenders, and crowbars, lumps of armoured cable for throwing, monkey wrenches, and giant adjustables. Someone flashed a Samurai sword. You wrote about all this shit in Ultra Violence, didn't you? Saturday afternoon entertainment for the common man. Samurai swords and lump hammers? Bear in mind, he had done basic military training when he was a kid. A professional killer, like all of them, and here he is – and he told me this – thinking, shit, I am SO out of my fucking depth, it is NOT true. He didn't describe the fighting to me – and there was some, on that wasteground, bad fighting, ultra-violent fighting – but I do know that he came back to Notts afterwards and left Stoke City behind...

Stoke are a force of nature, alright. Same as Birmingham, HobNob said. A Forest lad I grew up with had his throat cut on a Zulu wasteground.

Mini-Beefy sat listening to this and piped up.

I'm glad I follow Notts, dad. That's over the top. I can't believe it.

Really, Doubting Thomas? Go and ask Renfield if it's true.

Don't think I'll bother, dad, he replied.

Watching the last few minutes of the contest from the stands, HobNob was riling Mini-Beefy about running on to the pitch to celebrate the climax of the season, but his son felt he was too old at sixteen. Bull had his camera ready, like Bury in 2006, when Notts came close to the Conference trapdoor. A nine year old Beef ran around the pitch dementedly. Same as Torquay away, when Notts celebrated the Munto promotion. Beef found himself on the other side of the stadium in a mass throng underneath the director's box.

They were good times for everyone, memorable times. Running onto the pitch was something for the kids to enjoy, but Chairman Trew was having none of it this year, a ring of stewards and coppers circling the perimeter.

Clifton Tom came over to HobNob and tapped him on the shoulder.

When was the last time you saw as many coppers as this at the Lane?

Man City?

There's more than that here. My lad, Tony, is over there, look. He's trying to get on, but they aren't having it.

The perimeter was a sea of yellow, and it seemed that the entire profit from today's match had been recycled into a dogma of security. It was Chairman Trew's pitch, and he didn't want anyone running about. Besides, the pitch had been destroyed by a combination of a bad winter, the construction of the Pavis stand blocking out the sun's rays and the introduction of Nottingham rugby.

Hardly any grass grew on the right-hand side, and quality football this season had been at a premium. There may have been more rugby matches to come, for all I know (like most Notts fans, I pay no attention to rugby, a boring sport for the police, the professions, the middle class and their servants to enjoy), and it was obvious the chairman didn't want kids running riot on an already suffering pitch.

This left people frustrated: There was muttering, but in the end, the season had been so poor on every level, no one had any fight left, and rather than break through the cordon on the final whistle, the crowd stood their ground and the faces of hundreds of disappointed children was the final motif of a pointless end-of-season game. The Notts players circulated in front of the two stands (ignoring the sparsely populated Family Stand) and gave a round of applause to the crowd.

Neal Bishop made an appearance; some say for the last time, the last link between Munto and the club of 2013/2014.

HobNob stood behind me.

Bit different from Luton, huh.

I wasn't there, I replied.

That was worth coming to.

You told me.

And Bristol Rovers. Football was different back then. This is something else, and it will eventually kill Notts.

Why?

Apart from kicking the fuck out of that lot – HobNob pointed to the Coventry fans saluting their lemon-clad players in the Jimmy Sirrel stand – running on the pitch at the end of the season is the only chance these kids get to *interact* with the club. These stewards stop the lads standing up in the Kop and have killed the atmosphere. They blame health and safety, and they blame the City Council, but it's actually down to the stewards. Pointless fat cunts, too thick to join the coppers. Pub bouncers.

Why the City Council?

He looked at me askance. I told you before, they hate Notts. They want us out of their City, and they want their beloved Red Dogs in. We're a hindrance. I've seen plans for an Eastside development that doesn't have Meadow Lane stadium on it.

That's just paranoia, I ventured.

He laughed. That's what the British politicians said to the press when Hitler invaded the Sudetenland. They carried on believing his good intentions, but the whole population was wise to it. They were in on the gag from the start.

I had no answer to HobNob's conspiracy theory, and it was pointless arguing with a cynic, especially one who was also a zealot. I stood, applauding the players dutifully like a sheep, even if they didn't deserve a single clap.

Most of them wouldn't be anywhere near Meadow Lane next year.

Some Coventry fans were trying to get on the pitch, but the stewards surrounded them and coppers ran the full length of the perimeter to back up their brothers in arms.

HobNob, realising that I wasn't going to continue the conversation about the City Council, carried on his previous theme stridently, pointing out the crowd in a wide sweeping gesture.

The message is simple: Pay us all your money, sit down, shut the fuck up and watch the "entertainment". It's not like the old days. Terraces. Chanting. Standing next to some pissed up cunt with the breath of a thousand pies. Everyone ran on the pitch at the end of the season. It was tradition. It was part of it. Great atmosphere. Fucking great atmosphere, he said, wistfully.

Bull tapped him on the shoulder. Stop boring every fucker and let's go to the pub.

Have to take Beef to the bus, he replied.

I'll meet you in there. Beef, I'll see you next week. Enjoy your party.

Cheers, uncle, Mini-Beefy replied. The two shook hands. I said my goodbyes and followed Bull down the stairs. I had a feeling that following the younger Bully brother was going to be more interesting than watching father and son at the bus stop. Crowds swept toward the gates of the Pavis stand, giants in wrought iron. The atmosphere was benign and light, without being exuberant. I looked behind me. Tommy's Bar was heaving. I asked Bull where we were going.

Well, he replied. Either we'll bounce up and down to the Madness tribute band with the Trews and the civilians in the Meadow Club or we'll go to see what's happening in the Navigation. Which would you rather do?

I've never seen a tribute band, I said.

Is that something to be proud of?

I thought about that question for a while as the crowds emptied onto Meadow Lane.

Yes, I believe it is.

Let's fuck off to the Navi, see who's about, he said, grinning, slightly drunk, talking louder than he usually did.

Ten of them.

Seasoned lads from the seventies and eighties.

Coventry.

All the gear, all the disconsolate colours of the urban winter, Town Centre camouflage, spacious hoods, like monk's cowls, hiding baseball caps.

In the centre of the pub, right in front of the bar.

One lad in his forties, a two day growth of black beard, skeletal, emaciated countenance, stared at Bull, who stared back. I went to the bar and ordered the drinks, but there was a lockdown. The gorgeous little blonde students who populated the Navigation bar space knew there was trouble afoot. They could picture it. In their coal-black blouses, tidily dressed hair, shining like beacons in the night, sparkling eyes, handpicked by the old school management for their effervescent Scandinavian beauty, they watched the scene unfurl before them. The pub was packed. A half-moon design with two back rooms attached, standing room only as the drinkers watched the Sky screens for news of miracle escapes and despairing relegations into oblivion.

A bloke I knew as Steveo, in another unfeasibly green kagoule, was behind me, talking to Bull, who had not taken his eyes off Blackbeard, his back up on the bar.

These Covvo bastards have been walking round the pub elbowing people, staring them out. They're well up for it.

I can see that. How many we got?

They're all dancing in the Meadow.

Bull turned round. Steveo had three mates with him, one a bruiser from Forest. The rest of the pub, civilians and civilian Coventry.

Four of us. Fair odds, Bull said.

Suddenly, the oldest Coventry hooligan in a tartan baseball cap, called someone a scab cunt. It was audible.

(Scab cunt)

174

I heard it.

Bull heard it.

Steveo heard it.

(*Scab cunt*)

Who's a scab cunt? Bull said, putting down his pint of Thor's Hammer cider. He couldn't help himself.

This is what he did.

He could lose everything if the coppers came in now and I tensed on his behalf, gripped the wall. All the big cash. His family. His fast growing reputation as a go-to problem solver in the nuclear power industry.

All that gone ... all of it. He shouldn't have been anywhere near this situation, and there he was.

Those eyes flashing.

It was definitely going to go off. The old Coventry fan had lit the fuse, and we were outnumbered.

I felt my heart begin to beat faster, and my head start to empty.

Should I run?

After all, I was just the *writer*.

Bull and HobNob could tell me how it transpired later in the pub or in the Queens Medical Centre. Bull and the scabshouter were arguing from a respectful distance, though the comment wasn't aimed at him. The debate, not loud, more like controlled talking, took place just above the crowd's level of perception. Most of the drinkers carried on talking or watching Jeff Stelling. You had to be in the centre of it with your pint like I was. Right in the centre, the pub buzzing, the staff watching – for the second time today, I saw a manager reach for his mobile phone.

(Who's a scab cunt?)

(You are, you Nottingham bastard.)

(No pits in the West Midlands, you fucker.)

(Who's a scab cunt?)

Blackbeard had tensed.

Another Coventry in a beige kagoule, young, lanky, handsome, who looked like Levis from earlier, put down his pint. Yet another, dressed in the style of a modern rap gangster, even taller, with both a monk's hood *and* a Yankees cap underneath it, stood behind the old man with

175

the attitude. It may have been his son. I didn't like the look of him at all, especially as he had a slash on the left-hand side of his face.

(How old are you? You should know better.)

(What's it matter how old I am! You County cunts are all scabs.)

(I've never scabbed in my life. No pits in Coventry.)

(Scab.)

I felt the tension ramp, and I looked outside the window.

Sunny, the occasional Notts fan walking past on the way home to his family.

A couple holding hands.

A family of five heading over the canal bridge for an evening of Talented British Apprentice Masterchef Ice Dancing On Roller Skates and a takeaway pizza from Dominos (stuffed crust, coleslaw, super-large, two-for-one, an extra slice for dad).

What was conspicuous was the absence of:

a) Notts hooligans currently dancing away to an imitation version of One Step Beyond in the Meadow Lane Sports Bar

or

b) Coppers

Should I fight?

I thought about it.

James Cannon. 1880. There are only two responses an organism can make in response to danger.

Flight or Fight.

(Why you got such an attitude?)

(Coz I don't like fucking scabs like you.)

(I'm not a fucking scab…you should act your age.)

I could feel Bull's ire emanate. I knew he was going to explode.

Flight.

Fight.

Run.

Hit.

Hide.

Under the table.

Everyone moved forward from their positions.
It was going to go off.
It was going to go off
Glasses picked up.
Pub fights.
The worst.

Glasses smashing, urban grenades, shards of crystal, plasma, jeroboams, contusions, cuts, slices, flapping skin folds, long deep slashes leading to long deep screams, screams, screams.
No, no, no, I didn't want this.

(You're a scab cunt.)
(No pits in West Midlands, you Birmingham cunt.)
(I'm not from Birmingham.)
(You may as well be Villa, Coventry – suburban Birmingham.)
(What did you say?)
Bottles breaking on fragile skulls.
Man down.
Noses shattering horizontally.
Dental attacks, teeth shattered, sockets shattered, the screaming, the screaming, the screaming.
aaaaaaaaaaaaaaaaaaaaaaaaaaaaaaaaaaaaaaaaaaaaaaahhhhhhhhhhhhhhhhhhhhhhhhhhhhhhhhhhhhhhhhhhhhhhhhhhhhhhhhhhhhhhhhhhhhhhhhhh–the butting, the punching, the kicking, the gouging, the biting, the right hooks, the left hooks, the boots upside your head and the stomping on prone faces...
...my heart raced, and I nearly puked over a table. I looked up.

In the middle of the Coventry, a bespectacled black-shirted figure standing next to Blackbeard. Spiky black hair. Appeared from nowhere. I could see Bull grin. Blackbeard turned round, and HobNob was right in his face.
Bull moved forward, and the Clifton lads followed him...
...a flash of yellow to one side

…three giant coats, someone said.

(Fuck, they must be warm…!)

One pinned Bull against the wall.

Swear one more time and I am going to arrest you. Do not move. Stay exactly where you are, he said, and he said exactly that because I was standing next to him.

Relief swept over me like a silky wave.

(ThankGodthankGodthankGod.)

A policewoman intervened between Blackbeard and HobNob and another pulled him away to one side. Other Notts fans turned up and showed an interest. Whisky Jack appeared as did Renfield, Beech, Basford Paul, Little Dave and Big Eddie. The Coventry now completely outnumbered. Blackbeard tried to talk to Bull, offering handshakes. He tried to tell Bull that they had taken our pub earlier, but Bull told him that all they'd done was intimidate civilians and real ale beardy weirdies. Blackbeard was no stranger to this. He tried to shake hands with HobNob, but he refused and the two started staring each other out. Bull didn't care about Blackbeard – it was the scabshouter he wanted.

The coppers, one-by-one, marched the Coventry lads out into a van outside.

Bull and Blackbeard carried on talking.

What's that pub on the canal? Blackbeard asked.

Which one?

The Magic Spoons pub.

That's Lloyds Bar.

We're going there next, Blackbeard said, a glint in his eye.

So are we, Bull replied, stone-faced.

We'll see you there.

The policewoman tapped him on the shoulder, and he turned round and winked at her. HobNob blew a kiss at him. Blackbeard made a gesture, which seemed to suggest he wasn't impressed with HobNob's spectacles. The gesture seemed to suggest that those fashionable Buddy Hollies were in danger.

HobNob waved at him ostentatiously, attracting the attention of the coppers.

All quiet.

The coppers had (unfairly, according to some), ejected eight or nine beardy-weirdy Coventry drinkers who were enjoying a pint of the Navi's real ale while awaiting the appearance of Nottingham blues legend Ian Seagal.

Within two minutes, the pub had emptied of hooligans and rather than a bloodbath, a Saturday afternoon battle sufficient to smash one of the nicest pubs in Nottingham to pieces, order was restored. The sex-bomb blondes began to serve customers again, including the three of us.

I'm going down the canal, Bull said.

You've got plenty to lose. All of it. Leave it out. The Cov have been put on a train.

I want that cunt who called me a scab.

I know you do, but he's gone now. He's on his way down to the West Midlands.

Might not be.

Whisky Jack and Renfield piped up.

We're coming.

Another young lad in a black hoody nodded.

Me, too.

I guess I'd better come, HobNob said. But they won't be there.

Loads of little mobs of Cov about, Renfield said. It'll be a right nobble.

HobNob turned to me. You coming?

I nodded.

I'll watch.

You just watch, mate, Renfield said, not altogether as friendly as I would have liked.

10. Carnage and Poets

5.45pm.

As we walked over the canal bridge, five of us, the Polish car wash, the abandoned, boarded-up Globe and the ancient, dilapidated Indian in front of us, a combination of live reports and mobile phone calls provided us with a running commentary of the situation in Nottingham, which at times as we walked, resembled the communication lexicon of an overseas war zone.

Being an outsider, I wasn't at the nerve centre of things, the command bunker – Renfield with his push stick perusing the map, Bull with his, pushing the red chips one way, HobNob, the blue chips another direction, the maps on the wall, the pretty stenographers on the telegraphs and the typewriters. I was just a bystander, but I picked up what was going on, the Saturday afternoon entertainment on the last match of the league one season.

Renfield turned to Bull.

You know Jimbo?

I do.

He's just been at it.

He's sixty? He was sixty at Bournemouth. They had a party for him.

I know. Good, innit?

I overheard this conversation.

Sixty.

To this day, I would not have believed that sixty year olds fought at football matches, but HobNob isn't far off, only a decade and a bit away, and I looked at him, in his black shirt and full head of chestnut brown hair, trotting across the canal bridge, a man half his age. The sixty of my youth isn't the sixty of this generation, the health service performing miracles in keeping people alive. No more war, healthy eating, and health conscious wives with plenty of culinary ideas other than fish and chips. The end of cigarettes, changing genetic profiles, society's veneration of everything young and the incredible sense of the pointlessness of the modern world.

Sixty.

The more you looked at the issue of aged football hooligans, there was a certain amount of logic in it.

It was just a number.

One after fifty nine and one before sixty one.

Some Sikh geezer ran the London Marathon, and he was 102.

I know an eighty year old who runs ten kilometres a day.

Thirty years ago, sixty meant you were virtually dead, your shifts in a rice pudding factory a millstone around your neck. Weekends spent imprisoned in an armchair, your armchair, a seat to be avoided by everyone for more reasons than one; exhausted, watching a dead television with dead celebrities, dead themes, dead ideas, dead adverts, dead chat and dead game shows, drinking Double Diamond straight from the can, eating fish and chips (extinct fish, potatoes saturated in dead fat) straight from the racing pages of The Sun. Missus slaving, cooking and cleaning, transfixed by a reverie of hour-long Marigold fantasies involving fucking the smiling next door neighbour or sparkly shirted pub singers and eventually, Mr Sixty would nurture a streaky combover and his nostril gaps would swell like a pike's gills and his cheesy teeth would loosen: Tarnished eyes amidst sunken sockets. A scent sticking to him, a diaphanous presence the consistency of muslin in his faggy armchair on his faggy carpet with his faggy TV, and by the time he was sixty five and retired, he would be six feet under after a massive coronary and his missus of thirty years, before her month of grief was over, would be enjoying her next door neighbour's salty cock, her fantasies realised because her rice pudding husband was dead; she fancied her neighbour something rotten and luckily for her, those feelings were reciprocated.

Today, the sixty year old was off his armchair.

Having a good runabout in Nottingham Town Centre with his mates, his Hackett Cap and blouson, his hundred quid jeans, his Gazelles.

Keeping fit, keeping active.

A healthy regime for the modern age.
Gym in the week.
10k on the treadmill.
Five-a-side with the lads.
Salads and plenty of extra virgin olive oil.
No cigarettes.
No drinking at lunchtime.
No drinking in the week.
Kick fuck out of some know-nothing Cov cunt on a Saturday afternoon with the chaps.
No more armchairs any more.
All the heroes are on the streets.

Brentford in town coming back from Donny, pissed, incensed, disappointed, indignant, ready for it, drinking in the old Newmarket with the winos and the old men, attracting the attention of the pissed-up locals from the Dog and Partridge up the road, long-standing Forest, rough arses, men who would slit your throat as fast as tell you the direction to the bus stop; old school St Ann's pub fighters with skinheads and fading Stanley scars from eye-to-jaw, drinking since midday and spoiling for it, really, *really* spoiling for it.

Coventry had kicked off in the Blue Bell, an old time boozer transformed against everyone's wishes into a student paradise: Two-for-one, alcopops, vodka red bull, sparkly baby drinks, which didn't require an apprenticeship to acquire the taste: Staffy's mob, Levis, Jamie from Bestwood, that gang, scrapping like fuck off Parliament Street, not a hundred yards away from the off going down at the Newmarket, yellow-jackets everywhere.

Pissed up Forest in the Royal Children fighting on Maid Marian Way. Somehow, Leicester City have found themselves in Nottingham, a stag do, a birthday party and they're going at it like they're in a civil war or something outside the old Peoples College (a noble seat of learning, established for the edification and learning of the working classes, the sons and daughters of trade unionists, an aspirational dream).

Renfield laughed. One of the Leicester is dressed up as an apple, he said, and is being mashed underneath a parked car. HobNob, quick as lightning, said like apple crumble, and we all grinned, but not much, because there was fighting to do and the black comedy involved in street, pub and football fighting is only apparent afterwards, like that time Bull booted a Stag hooligan outside that Field Mill chippy and lost his loafer, the Italian shoe circling in the air like the raptor in *Kes,* everyone watching it in slow motion, watching it helicopter, watching it swoop, and because the filth were all over the situation like lichen, he had to hobble up the road to safety on one forlorn loafer, a purple and lemon-striped sock apparent to everyone in sight.

That was funny afterwards, in the Fountain, in the Dog and Bear, back in Notts, but not as much as with a hundred psychotic Stags in vans and motors up and down the A60 wanting revenge for a decent Notts off-the-pitch performance.

Whisky Jack gets a call from a mate.
The Coventry boys have been seen on Canalside.
Blackbeard. The Monk. The Scabshouter.
Whisky Jack nods to Bully, and it puts a spring in the step, and I start to feel it, the tension, and the nervousness. I knew full well that I wasn't going to avoid it, that I, like Hunter S Thompson, the Gonzo journalist, was going to be right smack in the middle of the action, right in the middle of it, influencing it, staring right at Schrodingers Cat, breaking all the rules, and I watched them closely as we walked into the Meadows, more like trotting than walking, the six of us.

Sooner or later, Bull said to his brother. It will be our turn, I can feel it.

HobNob had a beatific look, the type of expression that accompanies a religious conversion. Renfield had a similar look, but he's angrier, much angrier as if punching an away hooligan is a way of releasing some demon within, as if watching someone go down is a justification for his existence, as if he has slain a beast. Whisky Jack looks like Whisky Jack; sinewy, pinched, grim countenance, a phiz the colour of old candlesticks, the bridge of his nose encrusted with mini-eruptions, lifeless blood vessels, lumpy corpuscles, a traffic jam of booze and nicotine, and his eyes told me he's enjoyed far too many Saturday afternoons down at Meadow Lane.

He didn't look at me.

I didn't exist for him.

I was a passenger, a tourist, and he's going to kick the blue fuck out of someone, like it or not.

And Bull?
Bull laughs.
He thinks it's hilarious.
All of it.

Up ahead, near the pub, the Poets Corner, the top of the Meadows, Renfield spotted them.

That's them cunts, he said.

Instantly, without replying, without another word, everyone except me took an extra step forward and they were ahead of me by six feet. I walked on to the road, my heart racing.

There were ten of them, just standing there, not drinking, walking to the train station, having a look about, in the Meadows, sunshine bright, the wind dropped a little, a decent spring evening. The Meadows locals nowhere to be seen. I saw a wiry looking black geezer in a smart lemon hoodie at the head of them and a towering skinhead much taller than Bull. There was a man in a denim jacket with long hair, a rocker. Other troops in hoods and caps. They merged under the sunlight, and I also noticed they weren't running (that's a critical piece of evidence for me, one, which informed my heart and my bowels), and we were outnumbered by two-to-one, and while I was half shitting myself while life passed before my eyes, I realised that the other Notts don't care, *they don't care.*

They don't care about numbers.

They're used to this, being an ethnic minority in a town five-to-one in favour of Forest *(County's got no lads),* local gangsters who humiliate Notts *(little County)* and blacks who think nothing of leaving you minced and bleeding in the street for glegging at them funny, only you were *actually* looking at them because you went to school with one, and you wanted to say hello because he had been your friend (but he isn't now), and everywhere Notts go, they are outnumbered, a dying breed, the Wild Bunch coming out the whore sauna, let's go, says Pike and the rest say why not...

...dinosaurs, extinct, and the Coventry fanned into a line and trotted forward and we trotted forward and at that trajectory, I worked out that two little bands of Saturday afternoon funseekers would meet in about fifteen seconds, and it was going to be bloody, and I had a choice to make...

...HobNob turned round, that beatific, St John the Baptist on the Road to Damascus look on his porcine countenance, his eyes glinting in the sun, mouthing at me in silence, *are you in, are you in, it's about time* and I realised that I cannot run, I *cannot* run.

I cannot fight, have scarcely ever fought and have definitely not raised a fist in anger in twenty five years, maybe longer. I knew that my time had come and I raced ahead...

    ...and it went off, it went *off*...
    ...*(all around me)*...
    ...and I'm in it...
(the collision...the connection)
    ...and I'm out of it...
(on the deck...up again)
    ...and I swing, connect...
    ...I hear the screaming and shouting...
(cunt)
    ...feel the punch on my nose...
    ...connect again...
    ...silent shout...
(aargh)
(county cunt)
(little county)
(county's got no boys)

...feel the concrete pavement on my forehead, the kick in my kidneys...
...no pain...
...no pain...
...another kick...
(*get up, you're missing all the fun*)
...HobNob flooring my assailant, stunned look...
(*county's got no boys*)
...up...
...down, down, my cheek stinging, a slap...
(*filth, come on, run*)
...and Whisky Jack, blood pouring down his neck, helps me up, and we're running, and running, and running, deep into the Meadows while Coventry I notice, head towards the station, the Paddy Wagon unsure of who to follow, a yellow-jacket chasing us half-heartedly, gives up...

...an alley, the six of us, laughing, out-of-breath, old men, except the young runner, but I am buzzing, all I can hear is snippets...
...over in seconds...
...the runner flooring a big skinhead, HobNob spending his time saving me from giant rockers, Renfield chinned by their top boy, Whisky Jack headbutted, his nose dripping with blood...cauliflower ears and black eyes and standing your ground...and being sore in the morning, and they're all in form, and someone says I did well, that I cracked someone, and I look at my knuckles and I realise they are sore and I must have hit someone, but I have no recollection of that, none at all, and even as I type this, even as I recollect that battle in front of the Poets, I cannot recall my role in the altercation, but I can remember the time it took for the contusions and a serious black eye to fade, an eye I told friends and family away from Notts County came from a swinging door (hahahahahahahah, *poor you!*) after too many pints of Thor's Hammer.

Whisky Jack took a call.
He could scarcely stop the words from tumbling out of his mouth when he told one of his Newark Pie mates what

had cracked off. He said that Staffy and his gang were in town, at Squares, and they're up for a beer, all quiet. He said that he would be with them in fifteen. Bull looked round the corner at the end of the alley for the law, and he saw no evidence of it. He ambled back and wanted all of us to go and look for Blackbeard and his gang down at the canal because he wanted the Scabshouter, but no one was up for it – too many lawmen patrolling about with our faces etched into their consciousness. I looked at Bull, and he's disappointed. His brother didn't encourage him.

In the end, we all shake hands, and we split into three segments.

Renfield and the Runner.
Whisky Jack.
The Bully brothers and I.

The Should Know Better Club.

Goodbye, Notts County

We found a pub for a while, the Riverway, and enjoyed a pint and a giggle.

Let the coast clear.

No reason not to.

The coppers would disappear the minute Coventry caught their trains, their overtime at an end. Sitting at the bar, we were the only customers in – a typical night in a British suburban pub in 2013.

How do you feel? Bull asked.

I don't know. Numb. Calm. Elated. I don't know... strange. I've never done anything like that before.

Me neither, HobNob said.

We all laughed.

Seriously, did you enjoy it? Bull persisted.

I'll tell you when I write about it.

Is this going to be the last book about Notts?

There's that book I was telling you about. I replied, self-consciously.

About the FA Cup encounter at Rotherham?

That one. Not sure that it's enough for a full-length novel, however.

Crap day out, that. Forest nearly did Notts at night, as well.

When? Bull asked.

On Derby Road, the old Toll Bar. Sea Monster...

Fuckers.

New school...no one recognised them. No allegiances from town...no Notts mates. How it didn't go off, I don't know.

Anyway, I interrupted. There's *that* book...

Make it a novella, HobNob suggested, helpfully, ordering three more victory pints from the young barmaid who had spent the last fifteen minutes on her iPod IM system.

Might do, I replied.

It's even more fun getting away with it, Bull said.

What, than writing a novella?

No punching some away bastard.

Oh, yes. That. You took a big risk.

I know. I'm done now. I could have lost everything there. Been offered three years in Maracaibo. It could make me for life. I could have lost the lot. No more. Far too much to lose. No more demos. No more Navi. No more away matches. I'm done. That's me gone. That's me done, sir.

Yep, said HobNob. I'm going back to my life as a stockbroker for a fucking big bank.

You'll be in the Cedars again if you behave like you did outside.

I ain't *nevuh* going back there, motherfucker, he replied, doing a seriously bad impression of a gangster, modern type. His brother offered up his pint glass.

The three of us clinked, began to talk about something else until it started to get dark.

Then, it was time to go home.

Safety first – a leopard never changes its spots – we got out of the Meadows proper and onto London Road, and we walked down toward the Jury's Inn. Cars flashed by as we passed the old Norfolk where I first saw the lads in action. It was going to be a big night in town, I could tell, and I half considered staying out, taking in the Cookie Club or something like that, but I was getting tired. It was all too exciting for one day, and I had my notes to write up while they were fresh in my head. We walked quietly, the three of us surfing the border between pleasant drunkenness and being hammered. We'd been drinking since dinner, industrial quantities of real ale, Red Stripe and vodka. Occasionally, a minicab would stop to ask if we wanted a lift. We would always say no, but cheerfully.

Hey, Bull, HobNob said.

What?

Are you *really* not coming down the Lane next season?

Bull laughed. He was drunk now, the most drunk out of all of us. He laughed, and he laughed, and he laughed.

Why? Would you miss me?

Fuck off, you. It's Notts.

Would Chairman Trew miss me, I wonder? Bull said, and laughed even more.

Course, he would. He wants his money back.

And who would protect you from nasty hooligans?

Renfield, you cunt, HobNob said, amused.

On the other hand, there's Marky here. He's a hooligan now. How old are you.

Thirty something this year, I replied.

Thetty something, Bull said, adopting the Nottingham vernacular. Thetty something and no longer a Meadow Lane virgin. Hey, HobNob, he can look after you when I'm in Maracaibo.

Where is that, by the way? I asked.

Take the first turning to the left, just past Ripley, he replied, rolling.

Thanks…

Don't mention it.

HobNob laughed. I never thought of Marky here as a scrapper. He is now. You can fuck off abroad, then…

I'm going to be rich, brother. And then, you never know…

…what's that? HobNob replied, curious.

…I might BUY the fucking club...

...hahahahahahahahahahahahaha…

Now THAT, would be a real buzz.

It would keep us out of trouble, brother.

It would stop us hitting people, brother. We'd be too fat to run after all that pre-match carvery.

And curries, I said.

And those country famous pre-match curries, HobNob said.

You never know. We could all have a scrap with the other team's DIRECTORS! Bull said, rolling with laughter.

HobNob slapped his brother on the back. In that case, mate, I'll wish you all the best.

Besides, Bull continued, you can bring your new missus to the big game. It's the modern world. She's probably harder than you…who does she support?

Stags, but she doesn't go.

Convert her. You know what they say, HobNob.

What do they say, Bull?

Once you've been white and black, there ain't no going back.

You've just made that up, I interrupted, while the two brothers laughed...

I know, I know. I couldn't help it. Couldn't help it, Marky...

Walking down Station Street, past the Capital One building on the way to the Bentinck (presumably cleaned up by now), I noticed six or seven men walking behind us.

A crowd of them.

They appeared to have come from nowhere.

They didn't follow us up London Road, and I didn't see anyone when we turned the corner into Station Street. I know we were drunk and could have missed them. I wasn't sure. They must have come from up from Messiah House, the biggest hostel in the Midlands, and one of the biggest outside London.

Lads behind us, I said.

Bull turned round to look, chortling at his joke.

Chavs, he said. Maybe homeless. Harmless. Harmless Homeless. Don't worry about it. Are we having a last pint in the Bentinck?

It's shut, HobNob said. We blew it up with cake bombs.

And that, brother, is a crying shame as we well know, he replied drunkenly.

They're walking fast, I said.

Who? Bull said.

The geezers behind, I replied.

Then, we'll part like the Red Sea, my friend, here...Bull said, putting his arm round my shoulder, the first time he had ever done so. He reached into his wallet and pulled out a purple note...those unfortunate young men can have a good drink on me.

HobNob pulled out a fiver from his jeans pocket.

Yep, they can have halves on me, an all, he said, and the brothers laughed.

I'm not sure...I said.

They were almost behind us.

I could feel them, rather than hear them.

After all we've been through, Mark, you get shitted by a bunch of chavs! Bull said. He turned round to front the men.

Grim faced townies.

Homeless. Humourless.

Beards and earrings, painfully thin. An odour about them. A mixture of donated tracksuits and Gola trainers. A job lot.

I noticed that two of them wore white socks underneath shrunken joggers with elasticated bottoms.

There is a dog with them, but the dog is silent.

In the darkness, I cannot see its breed.

Bull, no, I said. This isn't right.

Oh, fuck off, he said. He stood still and opened his arms like Jesus, drunkenly.

Here, you lads! Any on ya fancy a drink on us?

One of them, a bearded skinhead in his fifties wearing a charcoal grey Adidas tracksuit and purple New Balance trainers, walked forward, ahead of the others. He started to chuckle, and his glee was convivial and welcoming.

Cheers, mate, don't mind if we do, and then stabbed Bull in his belly with a sharpened potato peeler.

(A shiv.)

(A shank.)

(A prison status symbol.)

Beard forced the weapon inside with such force that the bloody tip of the peeler emerged from Bull's back.

You could see Beard's yellowing, spacious, gapped teeth as he drove it in.

To make sure he achieved his goal, the homeless man twisted his whole arm round as if looking for something lost inside the trunk of a tree.

As Bull's expression turned from jovial laughter to abject surprise, Beard turned to look at us.

Thanks, lads, he said. I'm looking forward to a refreshing pint of Bishop's Mitre at my most favourite real ale emporium.

Shock hit me like a thunderbolt.

(he stabbed him)

(prison knife potatopeeler prison knife potatopeeler prison knife potatopeeler prison knife potatopeeler prison knife potatopeeler prison knife potatopeeler prison knife potatopeeler prison knife potatopeeler)
(stabbed him)
(dead)
(stabbed)
(Bull's dead)
(stab)
(prison knife potatopeeler prison knife potatopeeler prison knife potatopeeler prison knife potatopeeler prison knife potatopeeler prison knife potatopeeler)

A taxi drove past, seemed to speed up when he saw Bull go down on his knees; the shank, the shiv, a red stain spreading over the bottom of his polo shirt. He looked at his elder brother who was standing, watching his world change forever, as shocked as I was.

One word.

Brother, he said...

HobNob screamed.

NOOOOOOOOOOOOOOOOOOOOOOOOOOOOOOOOOOOOOOOOOOOOOOOOOOOOOOOOOOOOOOOOOOOOOOOOOOOOOOOOOOOOOOOOOOOOOOOOOOOOOOOOOOOOOOOOOOOOOOOOOOOOOOOOOOOOOOOOOOOOOOOOOOOOOOOOOOOOOOOOOOOOOOOOOOOOOOOOOOOOOOOOOOOOOOOOOOOOO and lamped Beard, a good one, flooring him, the back of his head crashing into the wall, but a black geezer in a cap, a New York Yankees cap, no bigger than a fourteen year old, who stank of piss, sweat, tobacco, and spermatozoa-coated boxer shorts, had already sneaked behind him, from nowhere, and with no warning, no threat, no possibility of appeal, ran a knife across his throat from his left ear to his right.

HobNob was dead before he hit the ground, his head half-severed, sinew and bisected blood vessels dangling onto his sweatshirt, ejaculated blood spraying surreal images of the Saints onto the walls of the old Capital One building.

I watched him die.

Bull struggled to his feet, blood flowing from between his fingers, but another man in a bright yellow safety vest and skinny jeans smashed him over the head with a crow bar and he fell back to the ground.

I watched him die, too, plasma dripping onto the pavement in pools.

I felt a carving knife at my throat.
Threw up my arms.
A stinky man in a claret and blue football shirt (*Hammers? Northampton? Burnley? Villa?*) searched me, and took my watch and wallet.

With a vacant look on his face, Beard walked over.
His breath.
Beer.
(A killer's breath)
Fags.
(Death)

I expected him to say something, but he didn't.
He just stared at me.
(Breath of death)
(Death of breath)
Something small and white wriggled in his beard; a scrap of paper, a Rizla offcut.
(Something organic)
I feel my bowels begin to expand.

Silence.
(He doesn't have to say anything, now does he, Marky?)
(2-0)

Predator.
Prey.
(3-0)
Hunter.
Slayer.
(final whistle)

The last thing I saw before passing into unconsciousness was the sight of his prison knife glinting in the streetlights and his face, his craggy, accusing

About the Author

Mark Barry, author of *Hollywood Shakedown*, the highly acclaimed *Carla* and the top selling *Ultra Violence,* is a writer and publisher based in Nottingham and Southwell. He writes extensively on a variety of topics including, horseracing, football, personality disorders and human relationships, but most recently, he writes about life in Nottingham and monitors closely its ever changing face.

Mark has been interviewed on several Radio chat shows where he has given readings of his work. His writing has been featured in the national press, and he has also been interviewed on television.

Mark resides in Southwell, Nottinghamshire and has one son, Matthew.